IBN 'ARABI
The Tree of Being

IBN ʿARABI

IBN 'ARABI

The Tree of Being
Shajarat al-kawn
An Ode to the Perfect Man

Interpreted by
Shaykh Tosun Bayrak
al-Jerrahi al-Halveti

Published by
Archetype
Chetwynd House, Bartlow
Cambridge CB21 4PP, UK

www.archetypebooks.com
first published in 2005, reprinted in 2012, 2016, 2019

ISBN 978 1 901383 11 9

British Library Cataloguing in Publication Data
A catalogue record for this book is available from
The British Library

Typeset in Berthold Bodoni
by Ian Whiteman/CWDM
Printed and bound in Great Britain by
TJ International Ltd, Padstow, Cornwall

I dedicate this book to my beloved wife and companion on the path to Truth, Cemile Bayrak:

In my care for you,
I protect you from my own eyes.
Perchance my sight hurts you,
I close my eyes.

By the name of the One who lit the heart's candle with the flame of life, enlightening the soul with thought,

The One whose great light shines upon this world and the next and through whose bounty Adam's plain clay produced a rose garden.

In the blink of an eye His boundless power shaped the universe, visible and invisible.

He had only to speak *Kun* (Be!) and all matter became.

This one potent word moved the Divine Pen, which drew infinite beautiful shapes and designs on the void's pristine tablet.

The sound of this one word created both worlds, including our father Adam's first mortal breath,

As well as the mind given Adam in order that he know the universe, in order that he seek and find all causes.

When Adam first saw himself as a being distinct from the rest of creation, he plunged deep into thought to discover what he was.

His thoughts traveled from his being out to the vast cosmos; then from the totality, his thoughts returned to this partial world.

The material world around was a fraudulent trivial thing, single,

like the number one, spread around, with all numbers being but its repetition. The worlds of matter and the spiritual realms were born through that single sound—breath. It came, and returned from whence it came.

But here, there is no coming and going back. If you watch carefully, you see that coming here is the route of your return.

Everything returns to its origin. Both worlds, one hidden from the eye and one seen, become one and the same, and are gone.

Praise be to God who is before all time, who decided the beginning and the end of the two worlds in one breath.

Both the world of spirit and the world of matter met at one point, where

the one became many, and then many became one.

You think things are apart, but it is an illusion. See!

The point moves so fast, you think it is a circle.

All mankind circumambulates this circle.

God's prophets are like caravan guides on this path,

And our master is the first and last guide to all guides.

Divine unity is signaled in the letter A of his name Ahmad, and

the M marks his name Muhammad. God's peace and blessings upon him,

the beginning and the end, the station at the end of this path.

He is the one who was told to say "This is my way! I call to God with sure knowledge—I and those who follow me."

And he is where God is, everywhere, visible to those who see by the light

emanating from his beautiful face.

He is ahead, and all men follow, holding his hand.

Those friends of God who are behind as well as those who walk ahead have given news of arrival at their destination.

When they become self-aware like Adam, they may reveal news of the Knower and that which He knows.

One of them dove into the ocean of Oneness and said, "I am the Truth."

Another rode in a boat on the same ocean, and told of

how near or far he was from the shore.

One looks at the outside and talks of dry land, while gathering shells,

and the other plunges into the ocean and gets the pearl.

One starts talking about the bits and parts of things, how they appear and function,

Another begins telling of the Eternal One and then of creatures who live and die.

One speaks of long curls of hair, the beauty spot, the curves of her eyebrows, the beloved man in dim candle light, passing a goblet of wine.

The other speaks only of himself and his opinions.

And the other loses himself in idol's love, identifying himself with the monk's rope around his waist.

Each one speaks the language native to the level he has reached, and it is hard to understand what he says.

You the seeker of understanding, you must strive to learn the meaning of what they say.

From the *Gulshan-i Râz* of Shabistari (1317 CE)

11

I wish to acknowledge my gratitude to my dervishes *Hajja* Rabia Harris, who reviewed the manuscript; my wife, *Hajja* Cemile Bayrak, who checked the English and made corrections with careful attention to important details; and *Hajja* Guzide Celestin, who typed it. May Allah be pleased with them.

CONTENTS

FOREWORD

O seeker who wishes to find salvation, the first thing you must do is to search out a master who will see your faults and show them to you. You may travel far and wide trying to escape yourself, but it is a master who will save you from slavery under the tyranny of your ego. Do it now, because whatever one has now is better than the best one imagines one will have tomorrow.

When you find him you must behave like a dead body in the hands of the one who gives it its last ablution. You must be ready to accept your master as he is. Never criticize or find any fault in him, even if he acts against religious canons. No man is faultless. All men err and sin and are not safe from wrong. You are not a judge seeking someone guilty; you are someone guilty seeking a judge who is just.

Do not hide anything from your teacher, an idea or an intention, be it bad or good. Do not ever sit where he sat. Do not wear anything he wore. Place yourself across from him with dignity and good manners, like a slave in front of his master.

When he asks you for something or orders you to do something, open your ears and use your mind to understand exactly what he wants. Don't do anything without being absolutely sure that it is what he willed. Don't seek the reasons why he wills what he wills.

If you have to ask something from him, do not expect or insist upon an answer. You must tell him your dreams, but do not insist on an interpretation.

Don't listen to people who talk against him, for it

will produce opposition to him within you. If you know people who oppose him, leave them alone: neither fight with them nor keep their company. Leave them to God, who will see to them.

Love those who praise your master and serve their needs as you would your own. If your master divorces his wife, don't ever marry her or have anything to do with her. Even with the best of intentions, never enter his house without his permission.

You must stay as close as possible to him without making yourself noticed. If he wishes to consult with you do not ask any questions or enter into discussion with him. Do not wish anything that he does not wish. If something comes to mind, keep it to yourself; do not exteriorize it. Follow the path he has indicated for you. It is thus that you will keep your noble station, the station achieved by the dignity of good behavior. That is the tie between you and him.

When you consult him about a matter concerning yourself, do it if he approves, do not do it if he disapproves—but if he told you to do it and gets angry at you for doing it, stop doing it. This change of mind is for your good, yet he will regret it. Remembering later that you bore no fault in it, he will find himself responsible and feel pain. He will try to repair what he did to you and at the same time you will keep your dignity and your good conduct. Beware: bad feelings toward the master are only found in students who are lazy, who do not do what they are supposed to do, and had the wrong intentions to begin with.

Don't oppose any of the master's actions or ask his reasons. Always be obedient. Be humble towards students whom your master favors above you. Even in his absence, sit properly, stand properly and talk properly in accordance with good behavior, as if he were there and looking at you. Do not walk in front of him unless it is dark. Do not look him in the eye—if you do, it will reduce your respect for him and take the beautiful feeling of shame from your heart. Don't sit in front of him unless it is necessary, but wait behind the door, so that you can be there immediately when he wants you. Do not go anywhere, even if it is to visit your father, without his permission.

When you come into his presence the first time, kiss his hand and remain standing until he asks you to sit. Protect his property. If you bring him something to eat, bring what he likes, in the amount he likes, the way he likes it. Don't stare at him while he eats. When he finishes, clear the table immediately. If there is anything left on his plate and he asks you to eat it, do so, for there is blessing in it. Don't be envious of what he eats and don't count his mouthfuls.

Work hard always; that is what will please your master. Always wish good for him and expect good from him. Yet beware that he may trick you, for sometimes masters purposely do this to test their students. Be heedful and very careful when you are with him. If you do something inappropriate in his presence, thinking that he will not see it, know that he sees it very well for he sees everything you do and whatever passes inside you. He merely pretends that he does not, because he does not wish you to be punished. On the other hand, if he chastises you and punishes you and hurts your feelings, accept it without resentment.

As long as he is pleased with you and approves of

what you do, your love and respect for him will increase. And as long as your humbleness and obedience toward him increase, your presence will grow in his heart and your state will improve. When your master is on a journey, keep the times when you usually meet him, and at the place where he sits, salute him inwardly as if he were there. It is not for you to ask him where or why he travels. When he consults you about a matter, know that he is not asking your opinion because he needs it, but as a sign of appreciation and kindness. Your answer should be, "You know best." Above all beware of opposing what he wishes to do. Even if you are absolutely sure that what he is doing is wrong, help him to do it and keep your thoughts to yourself.

On the Sufi path one advances only as one's master advances. Your hand is in the hand of your master, and the hand of your master is in the hand of God. Talking, discussing and interpreting are not going to get you anywhere. The path to truth is to follow instructions without interpreting them, for the understanding of secrets belongs to those who know them. If you say: "I think he means this or I suspect he wants that," trying to interpret your master's orders, you are really only trying to escape from doing what you must: best sit and cry over your failure! All disaster that befalls a student comes from interpreting the indications of the master. This all is the play of the ego. The mind, the true Reason, does not accept interpretation: it is not either this or that. There is an origin and a reason for every order; the true intelligence is anxious to fulfill it.

Even if you know what should be done next, don't do it or even think about it until your master so instructs you. Accept your master's every action, his whole way of living. The way he eats, drinks, sleeps, and behaves is his business, and you should have no opinions or comments on it. For your own sake, enter your master's life only when invited. Don't say, "Master, shall we eat together at home?" or "If you are not coming to such and such a place, should I go?" You are then trying to make him ask you to eat with him—indeed, to lie down with him! Instead of bringing you together, this will drive you apart, for it will decrease the love and appreciation and respect for you in his heart. If these feelings disappear, the tie is broken and that student will never find salvation or peace. Whoever says otherwise knows neither the path nor himself.

O seeker, see to it that your relations with your master are as I have described: may God so will. Know also that the beginning of this path is repentance. You must try to make even your enemies pleased with you. Forget their tyranny and shed tears for the time that you have spent fighting anything but your ego. Be a friend to knowledge: there is no one who is free from fault and sin. To make public accounting of the wrongs you have done in the attempt to show your master that you are repenting is in itself hypocritical and dangerous. The true sign of repentance is to leave what you have been doing, and from there on to be heedful, sincere, industrious, and pure.

On Worship

You must offer your five daily ritual prayers in congregation, and additional prayers at home. If you pray somewhere your master has prayed, do not stand at the place where he stood. Make a ritual ablution before each prayer, beginning every action with "In the name of God, the Compassionate and Merciful."

First wash your hands, intending to pull them away from the affairs of this world. Then wash your mouth, remembering and reciting God's name. Wash your nose wishing to inhale the perfumes of the divine. Wash your face feeling shame, and intending to wipe from it arrogance and hypocrisy. Wash your forearms trusting God to make you do what is good. Wet the top of your head feeling humility and wash your ears wishing to hear the address of your Lord. Wash from your feet the dirt of the world so that you don't stain the sands of Paradise. Then thank and praise the Lord, and send prayers of peace and blessings upon our Master, who brought the canons of Islam and taught them to us.

After you leave the place of your ablution without turning your back to it, perform two cycles of prayer out of hope and thankfulness for cleanliness.

Next stand in the place where you are going to make your prayers as if between the two hands of your Lord. Imagine, without forms and lines, that you are facing the Ka'bah, and that there is no one else on the face of this earth but you. Bring yourself to express your servanthood physically. Choose the verses you are going to recite, understanding their meaning within you. With the verses starting "Say...," feel that you are talking to your Lord as he wishes you to do: let every word contain praise. Allow time between the sentences, contemplating what our Master, the Messenger of God, gave us, trying to keep it in your heart. Believing that your destiny is written on your forehead, place it humbly on the floor in prostration. When you finish and give salutations to your right and to your left, keep your eyes on yourself and your connection with your Lord, for you are saluting the One under whose power you are and who is within you.

When you are entering a place, give salutations in the name of God internally and when you have entered it, bless it with two cycles of prayer.

On Eating

Eat the food a poor person would eat and leave the table without being full. Do not drink while eating and be sparing in the amount of water you drink. Do not accept special treatment while you eat; do not put on airs and affectations. Do not ever show your hunger. Measure the amount of food you eat so that you only partially satisfy your need. Your bites should be neither large nor small. Remember God at each bite, and chew well before you swallow. Each time you swallow, give time for the food to descend in your stomach and praise the Lord.

The practice of the faithful while eating is not to listen to the appetite of the flesh but to eat whatever is in front of one. Eating is a form of worship, so your movements should be controlled. Do not look right and left or think of your errors and shortcomings: be in a state of thankfulness. If there are people sharing the meal with you, avoid looking at them, at what they eat and how they eat, and try to be the last to serve yourself. If someone comments on why you eat so little, be polite but do not respond. If you explain and apologize, beware of being hypocritical. Do not leave the table until it is cleared. Eat only at mealtimes: to eat in between is gluttonous.

On Making a Living, Sustenance, and Satisfaction with One's State

Know this: If you forget the truth and do not apply it in your life, you will leave the path sooner or later, for forgetfulness of the truth shows lack of trust in God, and lack of the peace brought by satisfaction with one's lot. Trust in God shows your knowledge that you are unable to do anything by yourself, and that you know very little. Therefore you are humble; you count on Him, the All-Powerful and All-Knowing. That will give you peace of heart.

The evil of your ego may tell you: "So sit where you are, and let Him feed you!" To think this way is unlawful; fear it, for it is a sin. Do not listen to your ego, yet take care of its needs.

In this life you will have to be with others who push you as your ego pushes you, and there will be people of power among them. Try to be with those you know, for in this life it is hard to know who is a foreigner and who is a native. Don't settle in one place. Keep moving. Try not to know anyone or let anyone know you. If you find someone insinuating himself close to you or sneaking up on you, bringing you things, your ego will tell you: "It is God who has made him discover your need and put that generosity in his heart." Do not take what he brings. If you took anything, give it back, for that person has been watching you and is trying to buy you by satisfying the needs of your ego, not your true need. This is not sustenance sent by God. Even if you are about to die, don't accept this kind of gift.

If something unwanted and unexpected is brought to you, examine yourself closely, what you have and what you lack. If you feel pressure or discomfort in acceptance, do not accept that thing. Return it to the one who brought it. If, in addition to the feeling of discomfort, you also suspect that it is unlawful, neither accept what is brought nor the one who brought it.

If you feel no pressing hunger and if what is brought to you comes to you unexpectedly, if you feel no discomfort in taking it and if it is lawful, take the minimum you need and return the rest. However, do not stay in that place anymore. If the one who brought you this gift happens to be among the rich and powerful and insists upon your staying, leave. If he indicates to you places of worship where you could go, in lands where he has connections and influence, you need not refuse.

All these exercises will strengthen the truth in you. Know that if you do not follow this advice, you will be tyrannizing yourself.

Do not listen to the talk of the idle "Sufi," who sits and does nothing and says "My Lord is sufficient for me," for he has suffered all the things about which I have warned you. Do not be idle, for the best and the most lawful sustenance that comes from God is that which you have gained with your own two hands.

On Friendship

The hardest thing for the one who has taken this path is to keep old friendships. The student aims to leave behind all his old habits and all that his ego desires. Friendship, though, is connection and closeness. Of all things, to leave one's friends behind is the hardest and saddest. The one who wishes to come close to God must indeed distance himself from mankind. Yet when he does that, he is not necessarily with God—but he is necessarily alone. Worse, he may imagine himself to be with God. The best course is to distance oneself from one's habitual friends and tie oneself to one's master. One shouldn't even become too close to the other students of the master, or be with them against the wish of the master. Like a beast in the jungle, a student should stay together with his own species.

Those who wish to be with God and come close to Him should be independent of other people. They should remember, tie themselves to, and count upon God alone. When he is together with the other students, a seeker should feel that he is not with them, but with his master, and if he feels the absence of his master in the company of his friends, he should leave. If he feels no trace of the presence of his master in the conversation, and the conversation is totally secular and flippant, although it may be pleasant, he should escape from there.

The same applies to the clothes you wear. If you like your clothes and feel that they suit you well, sell them or give them away and buy yourself clothes toward which you are neutral. If you like your room or your house, change it. Keep giving things away and changing your place until you have nothing that pleases you, that preoccupies you, that captures your heart—until you feel that you are left all by yourself in this world without anything belonging to you. Know that God will not enter a heart where anything else resides.

A heart devoid of God is sick: if the student did not have his master as a doctor, that sickness would cause his spiritual death. Though the sick at heart cannot be with the doctor always, one must live very close to him, and when in need, seek his help. Still the doctor knows best when to see the patient, and the master, when to see his student. His purpose is to see the student's heart cured and renewed with the medication of remembrance of God and the diet of peace contained in trust in God.

If you get involved in something without telling your master and he knows what you are doing from your behavior, it is a sign that your heart has opened to him and you are truly attached to him—for he can read your heart.

Your relations with people should be gentle, generous, and sincere. You should ask nothing from them, knowing that you have no rights over them and that everyone is better than you.

The best thing is to have as little as possible to do with people. In any relationship people have rights over each other. If you have relationships with too many people and if you follow the right course in your relationships by giving them their due, you will not have much left with which to give God His due. If you are bankrupt like this, it is better to run away from the world and its demands.

When you separate yourself from the friendship of this world, if your friends complain about it, admit that you deserve their reproach. If they praise you for it, do not accept their praise; think that they see their own good qualities in you. If you do this, God will hide your real state from them. Woe to the one whose real state becomes visible to others! Remember that he who praises you is your enemy, because he is the friend of your enemy, and he who condemns you is your friend, because he is the enemy of your enemy.

Do not move around much. If you do, let your trips be of short duration. Too much movement is disruptive. It prevents you from advancing toward your real goal.

If you have to go somewhere, do not get distracted by what is on your right and what is on your left. Look where you are going; lower your eyes; watch your steps. Keep your mind on God and remember Him always. Do not stop to talk with this person or that, asking, "How are you?" or "What are you doing?" Idle talk! But if someone gives you salutations, return his salutations. If you see a believing servant of God, offer God's peace and blessings to him as if to all the believers in heaven and earth.

If you come across something that hinders your path, take it and remove it so that it does not hinder others. If you see something good that someone has lost, pick it up so that it is not trampled and put it somewhere visible on the side of the road. Show the right way to anyone who is lost. Help the weak. Share the load of the one who is heavily burdened.

Walk at a fast and steady pace. If you get tired, draw to the side and rest, being careful not to be in anyone's way.

Do not visit other teachers or participate in their meetings without the approval of your master. If your master permits you, you may go there to sit quietly and respectfully. Do not participate in their activities and ceremonies of remembrance, but do your own remembrance inwardly. This is better for you than to get involved in things you do not know. You may be affected by the hymns, the music, and the movements, and you may find yourself swaying. You may hear a hymn about death that casts fear into your heart, saddens you, and brings tears to your eyes so that you feel that life is passing, that the terror of death is near, and that there is a Day of Reckoning and punishment in Hell. All this excitement may seem like an invitation to get up and enter the circle of *dhikr*. Think twice! What is being said? What is being done? Who is saying it, what are his intentions? Is he sincere?

If what you feel is a separation from your senses, and from this world, then get up and participate. That is not a voluntary decision. You are not doing it for yourself; what makes you participate is something else. As soon as you return to your senses, stop and sit, and assume your previous state.

Moving in the ceremony of the Remembrance of God is a break from one's usual temperance and sobriety. Then one either soars above the norm or sinks under it. When you feel your movements and your physical body, you are in descent. If your descent continues, you end up under seven layers of the material world and sink into the conditions of Hell. If you lose your sense of yourself, of your movements, and of what is around you, then you leave yourself. Your heart ascends, filled with the might of Truth, to lofty celestial levels.

One is either in Paradise or Hell. Those who see you may think you are in a state of rapture, in communion with God, but that may not be the case at all. So it is best to abstain from participation in the religious services of dervishes of other circles.

If your need for friendship is too pressing, seek out friends who are sincere and righteous. Perchance you will find your master among them or through them. If you do not find such friends in the well-traveled quarters of cities and towns, seek them in lonely places, in ruined little mosques. What such people seek is in those lonely ruins, in deep valleys, or on top of inaccessible mountains. If you find them, try to be with them at the times of prayer.

The most inept seekers are those who miss the times of prayer and come to the congregation late. If you are late, even though you came, you did not come together with the ones who are there. Those who are delayed have been rejected by their guides. When you participate in congregational prayers, do not stand at the same place, or in the same rank, each time; even change mosques from time to time. Ask forgiveness from God for each moment of your life.

Befriend and be close to the poor. Serve them, help them, remember them, and think about them and their needs. Your consideration of them, your thoughts about their needs, are like honorable messengers coming from the One who protects them. How can you refuse to honor such messengers? So do what they need to have done; cook for them, clean for them, be a part of the good that comes to them. Then you will be part of what enters into their hearts.

Only good inspirations enter the hearts of the sincere and faithful who are needy, for their continuous battle with the desires of the flesh prevents them from having unclean thoughts. God Most High rewards them with both worlds for their trust in Him, and when you are with them, He will make you remember what they remember. If you remember and satisfy their needs, they will receive the rewards of their efforts from your hands, and you will be proving your own Trust in Him.

Is that going to be counted as a good deed? Are you to expect a reward? No! Yet do not belittle your action either. Your reward is that you have been brought to this path to truth, while the ones who negate Him are damned.

Whoever has these four attributes will be saved:

1. Service to the needy
2. Purity and peace of heart
3. Good will to the believers
4. Thinking well of everybody and everything

Keep these principles with you at all times. At the beginning, your efforts may not bear fruit. Your good deeds may be thrown back in your face, some by the people involved, some by your Lord. If you try to do good with an eye toward people's opinion of you, you will consider yourself farsighted, trustworthy, experienced, well respected, and you will end up thinking that others are inferior to you. Then know that the Devil has turned all your good deeds into evil.

The Devil's aim is to tire you, to trip you, to make you fall. He tells you that your lies are truth and that the truth is lies. He rewards you with unexpected gifts for your sins. Repent, take refuge in God, tie your heart to Him and remember Him always. He is the only one who can save you from the accursed Devil.

As long as you are sincere and constant on the path to truth you will keep the Devil at bay.

God knows best. May He keep you safe from the evils of this world and of your own self, and may He guide you on the straight path to truth. *Âmin, bi hurmati Sayyîd al-mursalîn.*

ON IBN 'ARABI

FOR OVER SEVEN HUNDRED years the world of Islam has been in controversy about the Shaykh. Many people love, respect and admire him, but there are also those who belittle and curse him.

Farsighted people of refined intelligence have always found treasures in the depths of the vast ocean of his words and have called him *ash-shaykh al-akbar* (the greatest of spiritual guides). But narrow-minded people, blinded by fanaticism, who cannot penetrate into his work, have insulted him by calling him *ash-shaykh al-akfar* (the greatest of heretics).

Great men have more enemies than friends. Even when our master Muhammad, peace and blessings be upon him, shed his light upon a world buried under the night of ignorance and corruption, only a very few welcomed him. Many, whose eyes were used to darkness, did not see his light—nor did they want to.

Ibn 'Arabi all his life felt the pain of not being understood. Yet the breadth and depth of his wisdom, insight, vision, and knowledge was and is awesome to whoever catches a glimpse of it. Many of his expressions of divine mysteries have never been improved upon. Many important affairs, which he foretold centuries ago, have taken place and continue to take place.

Despite—or because of—the controversy surrounding him, Ibn 'Arabi has become one of the most important expounders of Sufi wisdom. His influence quickly spread even beyond the Islamic world, entering medieval

Europe. In their famous studies, Asin Palacios and Salverda di Grave have pointed out that Dante, in the *Divina Commedia*, was often inspired by Ibn 'Arabi's works, deriving from them both the grand design of Hell and Paradise and the image of the beatified young woman as guide to the Divine. Through Dante's prestige, these themes permeated Europe. Today, the Shaykh's influence on the spiritual growth of humanity continues to grow as his works become more and more available in the West.

His words are like waves in an immense sea containing endless secrets. He produced through inspiration perhaps five hundred books. Many of them are short, about the length of a long article. Some, like *Fusûs al-Hikam, Mawâqi' 'an-Nujûm,* or *al-Futuhât al-Makkiyyah,* are books of many volumes that have responded to the questions and yearning of multitudes of seekers since his time. They are wellsprings of wisdom. Yet there is much thought in these books that cannot be digested by many people of intelligence—even scholars—if their intelligence and knowledge are not supported by pure and believing hearts. Nor is this wisdom accessible to theologians who see only the surface and the form of their religion.

In his prime, Ibn 'Arabi was a thin, middle-sized man—well proportioned, with small, delicate hands and feet. His skin was white. His head was small, with a round face, a high forehead, and a fine, slightly curved nose of medium size. He had eyebrows curved like the crescent moon; he wore a thick white beard.

He was courageous and tenacious, extremely patient, and very generous with both the material things he owned and the deep wisdom he possessed.

Although not everyone understood him, all were in awe of his spiritual presence. Always gentle, compassionate, and merciful, he viewed everything with love, including his enemies and dangerous animals. He detested violence, even in the punishment of murderers. He wrote, "Although according to religious law the punishment for murder is death, it is better to forgive." He also wrote, "On the Day of Judgment, I will intercede for those who deny me."

One of his contemporaries hated him so much that he would curse him ten times after each of his five daily prayers. When the man died, Ibn 'Arabi went to his funeral. Afterwards he wouldn't eat or drink or see anyone for days. A close friend insisted that the Shaykh come to his house for dinner. He obliged, but neither spoke nor ate, until all of a sudden, he smiled and started eating. When his friend asked him about his recent state, he said, "I vowed to my Lord that I would go into retreat and fast until He forgave that man who hated me so. Now, Allah, in His mercy, has forgiven him, so I can return to the life of this world."

Muhyiddin Abu Bakr Muhammad ibn 'Ali ibn al-'Arabi was born on August 7, 1165 (560H), on the twenty-seventh day of Ramadan, in the city of Murcia in Andalusia. He was a descendant of Hatim at-Ta'i, the legendary model of Arab generosity.

Ibn 'Arabi's father saw the potential in his son early, and when the family moved to the great cultural center of Seville, he had him thoroughly educated. At eight years of age he began to study hadith, Qur'anic commentary, and Qur'anic recitation with the famous teachers of the time. He also studied the literary arts and physical sciences and associated throughout his youth with many Sufis, including two distinguished female spiritual guides. At a very tender age he thus became accomplished in both worldly and religious knowledge. Even his teachers respected the intelligence and wisdom of this child.

Once his father sent the youthful Muhyiddin to visit the greatest philosopher of the era, Ibn Rushd (Averroes). Ibn Rushd was amazed by the supernatural talent and aptitude of the young man. He received him with respect and even debated with him. During their interview Muhyiddin was able to answer questions whose answers were only known to Ibn Rushd. Ibn Rushd was amazed to see that this young man knew things, instantly and miraculously, that he himself had only obtained through years of study. It was as if the youth were reading his mind. He said that, having read that such people existed, he was thankful to Allah for bringing him such a being. Still, the great philosopher, proud of his knowledge, was unable to see his young guest's true value and continued in his own way.

For his part, Muhyiddin wished to encounter Ibn Rushd again. In his dreams, though, he saw veils between himself and the philosopher; he understood this to mean that there was no way for understanding and agreement to exist between them. So another meeting never took place. When Ibn Rushd died in Marrakesh in 1199 (595H), his body was sent back to Cordoba. Ibn 'Arabi was there, and he observed with sadness that the transport camel bore on one side the coffin of Ibn Rushd, and on the other side, as a counterbalance, the books the philosopher had written.

While Muhyiddin was still a youth, he also made

the extraordinary acquaintance of Khidr, a wandering immortal sent by Allah to assist his special friends. Since the young man himself was destined to wander for much of his life and had unique access to hidden things, many people came to believe that the cryptic Khidr was Ibn 'Arabi's special patron.

In 1201 (598H), when his father and mother had died and his first marriage had concluded, Muhyiddin left Seville, intending to perform his Pilgrimage. He never returned to Spain. The Shaykh's journey eventually included all of North Africa, the Near East, and Anatolia. He visited Marrakesh and Fez in Morocco; Algeria, Tunis, and Egypt; Mecca and Medina on the Arabian Peninsula; Syria and Iraq; and the cities of Malatya, Sivas, and Konya of the Seljuk Empire. He traveled, in fact, through the entire Arabic-speaking world.

Before he left on this epic journey, he had a vision in which all the prophets were gathered. The Prophet Hûd advanced to meet him, and Muhyiddin asked him the reason for such a gathering. Hûd replied that the prophets had met together to intercede with Allah on behalf of the great Sufi martyr, Mansur al-Hallaj, who, as punishment for certain critical statements, had been kept apart for centuries from the Prophet Muhammad, peace and blessings be upon him.

In this vision Muhyiddin was also shown his whole life from the beginning to the end. This made him decide to start his travels immediately. His first stop was Marrakesh in Morocco, from whence a dream directed him to Fez. In his monumental work *al-Futuhât al-Makkiyyah* he relates the dream:

I saw a treasure under the Divine Throne where the verse "There is no power nor strength save in Allah, the High, the Great" is generated. I visited many other treasures under that one, from every corner of which beautiful birds flew out. The most beautiful of them all flew in front of me and gave me greetings. It was revealed to my heart that I should take it as my companion in my travels to the regions of the East. I asked my heart, "Who may this companion be?" I was in Marrakesh at that time. My heart told me, "He is Muhammad al-Hasar in the city of Fez, who begged Allah to bring him to the East. So take him with you as your companion." I was pleased with this, and told the beautiful bird, "Allah willing, you will be my companion." I went to Fez, sought and found him, and asked him, "Have you prayed to Allah for something?"

"Yes," he said. "I begged Him to send me to the cities of the East, and I was told that someone called Muhyiddin would take me there."

I smiled and said, "I am Muhyiddin." We became companions and friends until we reached Egypt, where he died.

During this period of his life, Ibn 'Arabi spent his time fasting, praying, and meditating. The last period of intense worship, which raised him to the level of sainthood, took nine months, from Muharram to the end of the month of Ramadan. He neither ate nor drank and was in a continuous state of ecstasy.

In Tunis on their way to Egypt, Ibn 'Arabi and Muhammad al-Hasar had a strange experience. The Shaykh relates:

> On our way, I found a man living in a marsh in a place covered with rushes. I learned that he had lived there for thirty years in seclusion. I stayed with him for three days. He prayed day and night and did strange things. Every morning he went fishing and caught three fish. One he would let go, one was his meal for the whole day, and one he gave to the poor.
>
> As I was about to leave, he asked me where I was going. I told him, "To Egypt." Tears came to his eyes. "Oh!" he said. "My beloved master, my shaykh, is in Egypt. Please go to him and give him my respects and greetings. Ask him to advise me what to do with myself in this world."
>
> I was amazed. That man had abandoned this world and the worldly. It seemed to me that he did not need any advice about it.
>
> When I went to Egypt, I found his shaykh living in a palace in complete luxury and wealth. He appeared to be nothing more than a man of the world. When I told him the request of his dervish in Tunis, he said, "Go and tell him that he should take the love of this world out of his heart." This also amazed me, coming from him.

On my return to Tunis I found the secluded fisherman and told him what his master had said. He shed tears of blood. "Woe is me! For thirty years I have separated myself from the world and spent my time in worship, but my heart still belongs to the world! While my master lives within the riches of this world, he hasn't a drop of it in his heart, neither its love nor its worries. O Muhyiddin, that is the difference between him and me!"

This story related by Ibn 'Arabi became the essence for many who follow the mystic path. While others withdrew themselves from the world, trying to purify their hearts in caves and cells, Ibn 'Arabi and other Sufis following his example wandered the world, viewing the beauties of creation and finding in it the traces of divine power. They used the world as an object of meditation and remembrance of Allah.

Indeed, seclusion is like a hospital for the sick at heart. As one does not stay in a hospital forever, neither is it right to stay in seclusion for more than a short while. Perfecting one's humanity comes through living together socially. At best, seclusion is necessary to clean the mirror of one's heart—which then must be taken out to the world, where the manifestation of divine power reflects on it and brings knowledge of the Creator.

When Ibn 'Arabi came to Egypt, he met most of the scholars, wise men and sages there. The *qutb*—the chief saint of the time—was also in Egypt. Ibn 'Arabi found him, for he knew that the perfection of his mystical growth depended on divine knowledge manifest in such saints rather than in only praying and fasting and withdrawing from the world. He relates his encounter with the *qutb*:

> One day the *qutb* asked to have a feast prepared for the community of sages in Egypt. We had made a meat dish, which cooked for a long time in large earthenware pots. After the food was brought to the tables, when everyone had taken one mouthful, all the pots broke. Suspecting a divine sign in that strange event, the *qutb* addressed us, saying, "What do you think is the reason for this strange happening?"
>
> Many answered giving physical reasons, and some, theological ones. One comment interested the *qutb*: someone suggested that the pots were trying to say, "I have been honored by the hands of the friends of Allah who came close to me. That is sufficient for me. If I hadn't destroyed myself I would have risked that the enemies of Allah might cook onions and garlic and leeks in me!"
>
> Then the *qutb* turned to me and said: "O Muhyiddin, what do you think?"
>
> I said, "The pot is telling us, 'May your heart break in a thousand pieces if you put in it the love of others after the love of Allah has entered it!'" The *qutb* smiled and approved and said, "That is exactly what I think."

Thus spiritual knowledge and the divine wisdom obtained through it bring one close to the truth, enable one to see the inner reality, and grant the ability to take lessons from everything one sees.

Ibn 'Arabi went on to Mecca, where he stayed for several intensely visionary years. Here he encountered his female image of knowledge, the young girl Nizam, "a sage among the sages of the Holy Places," who inspired his famous poetic work *Tarjumân al-Ashwâq* (The Translator of Ardent Desires). Here, too, he married again: to Fatimah bint Yunus, daughter of the *sharif*; and fathered a son, 'Imaduddin, who would follow his father and eventually, in 1269 (667H), share his tomb.

In Mecca he also began his monumental work, *al-Futuhât al-Makkiyyah*. The *Futuhât* is a vast compendium of insights and unique symbolic teachings; each of the eight volumes took a calligrapher two years to copy. What it contains is not knowledge obtained from university scholars or written in books, but wisdom revealed from divine sources, discovered through personal experience. When he was writing it, it was as if he were forced to do so against his will. He became feverish and would sweat, even when it was cold. He confessed, "I do not write literature out of my own will and intention, as others do, but I receive such powerful inspiration that it burns my very being. Only writing it down extinguishes the fire."

For instance, he relates in the *Futuhât* an inspiration he received:

As I was circumambulating the Ka'bah I saw a strange person, quite different in appearance from what I was accustomed to seeing among

42

the people. As he walked around the Ka'bah he continually recited, "We, like you, are circumambulating this House." I caught up with him and asked him who he was. He said, "I am your ancestor far removed."

"When did you live?"

"I died over forty thousand years ago."

"They say Adam, may Allah's blessing be upon him, was the first man and lived only six thousand years ago."

"Which Adam do you mean? Know that he is only the last of one hundred thousand Adams who came and passed away before him."

(Indeed, modern science has discovered evidence of people who lived hundreds of thousands of years ago. There is no indication in the Holy Qur'an, nor in the *hadiths*, that man was created seven thousand years ago. This idea came from an interpretation of certain genealogies attached to the Torah.)

The Shaykh relates another such incident that occurred in Mecca:

One Friday, after the congregational prayers, I was circumambulating the Ka'bah. I saw a man whose costume and physical appearance were very different from those of everyone else. He seemed to be floating in the crowd, passing in between people without even touching them. It was revealed to me that he was a pure spirit made visible.

I stopped and greeted him and talked to him. His name was Ahmad as-Sabti. I asked him how it was that he was given the privilege of assuming a form and shape and of performing the *hajj* after having left this world. He said, "I used to work for this world only one day a week, for my sustenance. I spent the rest of my time in worship."

"Which day did you work?" I asked.

"Saturday," he said, "because Allah Most High began the creation on Sunday and ceased working on that day. So I worked the day He ceased work, and received the profit of the six days He worked!"

"Who was the *qutb* when you were in this world?" I asked him. He said that he was. Then he disappeared.

A Meccan friend of mine who was present asked me, "Who was that person who talked to you? I have not seen such a person in Mecca all my life!"

As Hafiz ibn Najjar has said, "Ibn 'Arabi was a *qutb* and knew the other *qutb*s of his time. Furthermore, he knew the *qutb*s of the past and future. Mostly he kept company with the Sufis and spent his time at the Ka'bah. That seemed to be his only pleasure."

Despite his deep attraction to the Ka'bah, his business in Mecca was temporarily concluded two years later and he resumed his travels. In the year 1204 (601H) Ibn 'Arabi came to Baghdad. He stayed only twelve days. In that brief time he found and wore the cloak that had been left for him fifty years before by the pivotal Sufi teacher Shaykh Abdul-Qadir al-Jilani, and he met with the wise men and sages of Baghdad. He spent another three years on the road, in Mosul and Egypt, before returning to Mecca in 1207 (604H).

This time he could spend only a year in Mecca before the journey summoned him. He returned to Mosul, proceeded through Malatya and Sivas, and came in 1210 (607H) to Konya, the political and cultural capital of the western Seljuk empire. In Konya he is believed to have married the widowed mother of Sadruddin al-Qunawi. Sadruddin was the grandson of the sultan of Malatya and already a promising Sufi. His intention in this marriage was more than having a good wife; it was also to have as a son Sadruddin, who later became one of his most important disciples.

(The Shaykh's other blood son, and his daughter, were possibly born from this marriage. Sa'duddin, born in Malatya in 1220 (617H), devoted his life to the study of hadith and died in Damascus in 1258 (654H). His beloved daughter Zaynab probably died while still a child.)

Ibn 'Arabi came back to Baghdad in 1211 (608H). Here he encountered another great Sufi shaykh, Shihabuddin 'Umar as-Suhrawardi. When they met, they meditated upon each other without saying a word. Suhrawardi's opinion: "Ibn 'Arabi is the ocean of truth. Everything he is and everything he does follows the example of the Prophet. Both his visible self and his inner self reflect and are filled with the light of Muhammad, peace and blessings be upon him."

It was around this time that Ibn 'Arabi's mystical knowledge reached perfection. He was so immersed in the ocean of Truth that his words as well as his inner being became invisible and inconceivable to those who remained on the shore. From 1213 (610H) to 1221 (618H) he moved from Baghdad to Aleppo, back to Mecca, back to Malatya, and again to Aleppo. During this period he increasingly encountered envy and misunderstanding, much of which he attempted to disarm. Yet he also found supporters in high places: for example, al-Malik az-Zahir, ruler of Aleppo, and al-Malik al-'Adil, ruler of Damascus. When, in 1223 (620H) al-'Adil implored him to settle in his city, he accepted. His wanderings were finally over. Except for a brief visit to Aleppo, he would remain in Damascus for thirty years.

Since the event is said to have occurred in 1223 (620H), it must have been in Damascus that Ibn 'Arabi met a young man who would become another Sufi of universal scope and appeal, Mevlana Jalaluddin Rumi, inspirer of the Mevlevi Sufis, the famous whirling dervishes. (It was still five years before Rumi and his family, now wandering as refugees, would move to Konya, where Ibn 'Arabi's disciple Sadruddin al-Qunawi would later become attached to Jalaluddin as well.)

The adolescent Jalaluddin accompanied his father Baha'uddin (one of the greatest men of knowledge of his time) on a visit to Ibn 'Arabi, who recalled this meeting with pleasure:

> I asked Jalaluddin how old he was and he answered that he was a year younger than *Huda*, Allah the Guide. According to the numerical value of the letters, the word *Huda* adds up to 605. As Jalaluddin said he was a

year younger, he meant that he was born in 604 (1207 CE).

As Baha'uddin and young Jalaluddin took their leave, Ibn 'Arabi said, "Amazing, that an ocean is following a small lake!"

Not all of the Shaykh's encounters in Damascus were happy ones. Many of the scholars and theologians there, as elsewhere, envied and hated him—not least because he had the favor of the prince and his highest officials. Their claim, though, was always that his religion was suspect. One scholar who defended him was Kamaluddin ash-Shami. "Those of you who deny him and condemn him and claim not to understand him, come to me!" he offered. "I will speak in your tongue, help you in your difficulties, and eliminate your doubts." It is not clear that his offer was very widely accepted.

In his turn, Ibn 'Arabi was none too fond of the scholars of Damascus, but their opposition to him was not the reason. He disliked them because they sold their knowledge for profit, and that money had become a veil preventing them from seeing the Truth. He hated money, and he hated the people who made money their god.

Someone once gave him an enormously valuable palace as a gift. Immediately after he accepted it, a beggar came and asked him for money. He had none. "O man in need," he said, "I have no possessions except this palace. Please take it, for the love of Allah!" And he gave the beggar the palace.

One day in Damascus he saw an *imam*—a lover of money, not of Allah—leading a whole congregation of people who also had the love of money in their hearts. He called to them from the door, saying, "I am treading upon the god you worship; he is under my feet!" The congregation left their prayer to curse him and beat him. Some say he died from the wounds he received on this occasion.

He left this world on the night of Friday, November 16, 1240 (638H), the twenty-eighth day of the Arabic month of *Rabi' ath-Thani*. He was seventy-six years old. His funeral prayer was presided over by the *qadi* of Damascus, and he was buried in the quarter of Salihiyyah.

The scholars eventually had their revenge. His grave later became the site of a garbage dump. So it remained until the Ottoman sultan, Selim I, the Resolute, took the city of Damascus.

Sultan Selim believed that Ibn 'Arabi had predicted his conquest of the Near East and Egypt in an essay called *Shajarat al-nu'maniyyah fi dawlat al-'uthmaniyyah*, which described the Ottoman state long before it existed.

In that essay it was also written, *Idha dakhalassînu fish-shîn, yash'aru qabra Muhyiddîn* (When the letter 'S' enters the letter 'Sh,' Muhyiddin's tomb will be discovered). The learned men in the Ottoman court interpreted the letter "S" as standing for Selim and the letter "Sh" as the city of Sham, or Damascus. They informed the sultan that he would discover the saint's tomb when he conquered Damascus.

Indeed, when Selim entered Damascus, the first thing he did was to search. He found the lost grave covered with garbage. The great warrior wept and ordered a tomb and mosque built on the site. Then he commissioned Shaykh Makki, one of the greatest theologians of the time, to write a book on Ibn 'Arabi's life and works.

Shaykh Makki wrote *al-Jânib al-gharbî fî mushkilât Ibn al-'Arabî*, attempting to clarify some of the misunderstandings about Ibn 'Arabi's thoughts in a language even narrow-minded people would understand. Other scholars of the time were encouraged by the sultan to write forty commentaries on the *Fusûs al-Hikam*.

Sultan Selim also visited the mosque where the attack that may have caused the saint's death had occurred. He found the spot where the Shaykh had said, "The god you worship is under my feet!" and had it excavated. A treasure of gold coins was discovered.

May Allah have mercy on the soul of Muhyiddin Ibn 'Arabi, and may He be pleased with him and bestow peace upon his soul.

May the Creator of All, Master of the universes seen and unseen, known and unknown, Allah—free of all fault, heedlessness, defect and deficiency, pure and most holy, knower and container of all things, the Lord who preserves us from all disasters and calamities—bestow His blessings and grace upon our master Muhammad, upon his family and companions.

May Allah bestow His peace and blessings upon our Master Muhammad, upon all the prophets and messengers, upon the saints and the righteous servants, upon the angels, upon those who reside by the Throne of Grace, and upon all faithful servants among the peoples of the earth and in the heavens. *Âmin.*

◆

An Ottoman legal edict passed by

Kemal Pashazade, Teacher of Sultan

Selim the Resolute (1470-1520):

All praise is due to Allah who brought us to the level of knowledge and obedience so that we might pass a just decision, and peace and blessings upon His Prophet whom He has sent with divine instruction to correct the misguided.

We declare to all men:

Know that one of the greatest of all teachers, the leader of those who believe in divine unity, the Pole of Knowledge, the performer of miracles, Muhammad ibn al-'Arabi at-Ta'i, known as Shaykh Muhyiddin of Andalusia, is a perfect man who abided by all that Allah has sent.

He is a virtuous guide, legendary in his incredible miracles. He is responsible for the education of multitudes of men of knowledge, honored by all for their piety and virtue. Whoever denies him and accuses him of blasphemy is himself blasphemous. If someone insists on denying him the praise due him and continues to accuse him, it falls upon the sultan to punish him, as well as to insist that the condemned one retract his statements. May the sultan abide with this edict, a reflection of divine justice.

Shaykh Muyhiddin has written many books, the most important of which are *al-Futuhât al-Makkiyyah* and *Fûsus al-Hikam*. These books contain some material the content and expression of which is clear and understandable to all. Other material is veiled and kept secret from the eyes of people who only see the exterior of things. It belongs to those who are able to discover and see the inner reality. All of it is in accordance with the divine ordinances as well as the canons brought by our master, the Messenger of Allah, peace and blessings upon him. The ones who do not understand some things, distort them. Those who cannot understand these refinements should remain silent. They certainly should not accuse the writer of their own misinterpretations. I base my legal opinion upon what Allah, the Ultimate Truth, says in Surah Isra', 36:

> *Do not pass judgment upon that of which thou hast no knowledge. Otherwise your ears, your eyes, and your heart will hold you responsible.*᷎

ON IBN 'ARABI'S THOUGHTS IN HIS OTHER WORKS

The Purpose of the Creation of Mankind

IN HIS MONUMENTAL work *The Meccan Revelations*, Ibn 'Arabi claims that God created humanity in order to make Himself known. He bases his belief on the verse in the Qur'an where God says:

> *I have only created jinn and men that they may worship Me.*
>
> (Surah Zariyat, 56)

The great commentator Ibn 'Abbas gives the meaning of "to worship" as "to know", stating that the purpose of man's existence is to know God.

God has created everything in perfect order, connecting everything with everything else, and connecting, also, everything to Himself. He has manifested His attributes upon His creation, and regulates the actions of each thing in relation to the divine attributes bestowed upon it. Speaking through His Prophet, God says, "I was a hidden treasure, I loved to be known, and through this love I created creation." God has honored humanity, His supreme creation, with being a means of His becoming known.

Just as God's essence is incomparable with, and other than, His creation, so the human being has no equal in creation as a manifestation of all His most beautiful names and attributes. God is Most Perfect and has created humanity perfectly. The human being contains all of the potentials necessary for reaching the perfect state. As God is in need of nothing, He has made humanity in need of nothing but Himself. Thus God made man to know Him, and man is capable of knowing the truth and finding perfection.

The practical meaning of "worship" in this Qur'anic verse is to abase oneself, to erase oneself in front of the Lord. The reward of that undertaking is a conscious connection between the created and the Creator. It is a means of coming close to Him and knowing Him. The Lord says: "Pray to Me so that I accept your prayers."

In the same divine verse, not only men but also *jinn* are mentioned, because in the whole of creation there are none but men and *jinn* who, with arrogance, claim to be Lords themselves, over everything that exists. Nothing else in creation is given the possibility of ownership. Nothing else can inherit. Nothing else can call another of its own kind its slave. Nothing else can claim to represent God. Nothing else in the world is conscious, claiming to have life, power, and will—the divine qualities of Ever-Living, All-Powerful, and Total-Will, which belong to God.

The possibility of this claim is the meaning of "God has created man in His own image." These manifestations of divine attributes in man, so misused by him, are also the connection and the relationship between us and our

Lord, and a means for us to know our Lord.

It is in consideration of man's willfulness and arrogance that "worship" must signify self-abasement before it can mean knowledge of the Lord. For all the knowledge that human beings with their given intelligence can attain, is as nothing before God's infinite greatness. We must bow our heads in cognizance of that fact. It is only through utter humbleness that we will be able to realize the purpose of our creation. But it is also true that someone who does not know his Lord already is incapable of erasing himself in the first place!

How to Find God

The Creator can only be found through His creation. Everything is a witness to His existence. Without knowing the reality of reality, it is impossible to know God.

Avicenna, a contemporary of Ibn 'Arabi, claims that God can be found through rational thinking apart from the knowledge of His creation. Ibn 'Arabi says that the manifestation of God is in His creation and it is impossible to know Him otherwise.

Creation is continuous in the universe. Each event of creation is different; they are not repeated. The endless procession of uniqueness is a proof of the infinite divine power. Every new action is a mirror where divine attributes are manifest, and in every one of them there is a new and special knowledge. This is the only source of divine knowledge.

If we look at the heavens, we see a sign of the manifestation of God's attribute "The All-Covering Vastness." The seemingly immeasurable ocean suggests the divine attribute of "The All- Comprehending." Were we to contemplate our own life, and the living things around us, we would understand the meaning of "The Ever-Living God." Should we look upon a person of knowledge, we would remember "The All-Knowing God." In a doctor we would see the signs of "The All-Healing God." And if we considered the human being, we would see the evidence of "The All-Uniting God."

The human wish to find our Lord can draw us to see His manifestations in everything around us and within us. Then the whole of life and the universe becomes a book that teaches of the Lord, because every created being is nothing less than a manifestation of the beautiful names of the One who created it.

We will also be aware of things opposite to each other, contradicting each other: the manifestation of the divine attribute of "The Guide" versus the manifestation of "The One Who Hinders"; "The Beneficial One" versus "The One Who Prevents." In some moments of creation, one of these attributes overcomes; and in others, the other. Whenever "The Guide" and "The Beneficial One" are superior in quantity and quality, peace and prosperity are dominant. When that state decreases, difficulty and hindrance manifest themselves, and pain and poverty become dominant. This can occur within a single human being or in the whole of the world.

In this way a creation where good is manifest exists in opposition to a creation where bad is manifest. That is why the people who are bound for Paradise do not like the people who are bound for Hell, and vice versa. There are animals also in which beneficial attributes predominate, other animals in which harmful attributes are manifest. Both of these animal qualities are in every human being. Those who are overwhelmed by the nature of wild animals are much worse than the worst of the actual animals, while those in whom beneficence prevails are raised to the level of angels. The saint Mevlana Jalaluddin Rumi says, "O man, you side with the animal in you, and you side with the angel in you. Leave your animal nature behind so that you can rise above the angels!"

Thus humanity must know the manifestation of divine attributes in the continuous creation around us, and find its equivalent in our own nature—for God has taught us all His names. If we do this, we will know our Lord in His infinite qualities. But at the same time that we see the immensity and perfection of the Creator, we will see the minuteness and imperfection of the qualities manifested in us. Then we will realize our nothingness and our total need of Him. That is the beginning of the realization of the human being as the servant and God as the Lord, which is the purpose of the creation.

"He who knows himself, knows his Lord"

The truth of the attributes, the beautiful names of God, is infinite, and manifests in different ways at different times. The proof of Truth is in the realization of the oneness of all creation. Yet multiplicity is a part of the one. Unity manifests itself in multiplicity. With all their differences, and in the infinity of manifestation, the parts interconnect and add up to a whole. Whoever can find this in himself, knows his Lord.

God has created the perfect human being in His own image—in the image of His attributes.

Many Sufis believe that to be able to realize this

unity of the self, one must obliterate the manifestation of many "I"s in oneself—in fact, one must deny them existence. Through intensive worship, fasting, meditation, and refusing the desires of the flesh, they attempt to submit their wills to the will of God, and to purify their behavior and habits. All of this discipline and effort is built on the assumption that these many "I"s that one is trying to give up actually exist. Yet there is no "I" other than God. There is nothing but He. How can one manage to give up something that never was? The only way to know your Lord is by knowing your nonexistence.

Man is nothing but a mirror where God's attributes are reflected. He is the one who sees Himself in that mirror. He is the only one who knows Himself. Neither the prophets, nor the angels, nor a perfect human being can know Him. When we recognize our nothingness and God's totality, we attain the full scope of our knowledge of Him.

The Unity of Being

Three different approaches are necessary for understanding the unity of being. There is a unity of essence, a unity of attributes, and a unity of action.

The unity of essence is the concept that there is only one existence, one cause—inconceivable, unknowable, yet responsible for the existence of all and everything. The quality, the character, the attributes, the identity of all and everything are the manifestation of this one cause. Every existence is related to it, and every action of every created thing is caused by and connected to it.

Everything is from God, and yet is not God. He is before the before and after the after. He is the outer and the inner, the visible and invisible. His outward manifestation is the unity of everything, and still He is hidden in His Oneness. In the beginning, there was nothing but He. Right this moment, there is nothing but He. He is infinite—therefore, He will be when all is gone. His actions are unceasing and change constantly, no two are alike. Therefore there is none like Him, and there is none other than He. Whoever does not see this is blind in this life, and whoever is blind here will be blind in the Hereafter.

Mullah Jami' says, "Look at the whole creation under one single light, so that you will see the truth. There is only one light, but under that light different things are seen. The light unites all. This is the meaning of the unity of being."

That light erases the doubt and ugliness of imagination. The human being whose heart is freed of this ugliness sees the one, the most perfect, the most beautiful existence. There is no more harm, confusion, or deformity; all is right and true and beautiful. Such a one sees his own imaginary existence as a manifestation of the true existence, and thus passes from his existence to the true existence. He sees all humanity and all the created world as faultless, perfect, and beautiful, for truth is beautiful. And all is united in love.

Worship

God says:

> The seven heavens and the earth and all beings therein declare His glory. There is not a thing but celebrates His praise, but you do not understand how they declare His glory!
>
> (Surah Bani Isra'il, 44)

The earth has been entrusted with knowledge by God, as humanity has been entrusted with knowledge. The earth also knows its Creator. The truth is within everything. If man, with heedfulness, looked around himself, he would detect it immediately. God says:

> On that day [the earth] will declare her tidings; for that her Lord will have given her inspiration...
>
> (Surah Zalzalah, 4-5)

> Thy Lord has revealed to the bee...
>
> (Surah Nahl, 68)

> And He revealed to an ant the presence of His prophet Solomon.
>
> (Surah Naml, 18)

He tells us that a day will come when the earth will speak of all that has happened upon it. Things we presume to be without life will be witnesses on the Day of Judgment; thus, they know. A rock, although it appears inanimate, has a face turned to its Creator and a face turned to man. It is filled with the love and fear of God, while we think that it is senseless. We are senseless ourselves, living and walking upon the face of the world, believing it to be lifeless!

All creation has a language of its own, but no one, save those whose ears of the heart are open, can hear it. How else could the earth evolve into layers of elements—lead, copper, silver, and gold—into jewels and diamonds? Seeds grow into plants, into thousands of grains and fruits. Nothing is lost; everything is kept in the memory of nature. An ear like Solomon's can hear the words of the winds and the mountains and the birds.

It is reported by Anas, the companion and adopted son of the Prophet, may God's peace and blessings be upon them, that the Messenger of God took up some pebbles in his hand. A voice came forth from them, crying, "Allah, Allah, Allah!" When he gave the pebbles into the hands of his beloved companion Abu Bakr, the stones still kept reciting the name of God. But when Anas was given the pebbles, no more was heard.

One day the Prophet was ill. The angel Gabriel came to him in the form of a beautiful human being and presented him with wonderful grapes and pomegranates. As he was eating them, a voice proceeded from them, speaking the name of the Lord. When he gave some to his grandchildren, Hasan and Husayn, the fruits kept reciting the names of God, but when another of the companions was given the fruit to taste, the sound ceased.

The cognizance of the Creator is within the creation. This is the manifestation of God's name "The All-Powerful."

All that is taken to be lifeless matter—the earth, the water, the air, the fire—is immersed in continuous worship of its Lord. As a stone has neither mind nor thought nor feeling, as it is without emotion or will, it exists naturally in a state of complete submission.

The plants are in a lesser state of submission because they have a will to grow, and in their effort to grow they forget God and lack in worship.

Lesser still is the submission of the animal, the sentient being. Although animals do not have a fully developed mind and will, they have instinct, and that is what prevents them from total submission and full wor-

61

ship and realization of their Creator.

Man is the least apt to submit to God and the most lacking in worship. His mind, his imagination, his lust, the desires of his flesh, his anger, his will are the powers which hold him and keep him in heedlessness. At best, he may intend to know his Lord by his intellect, seeking proofs of His existence, wishing to see Him with his own eyes, and suffering under the influence of the will given to him.

It is only the perfect human being who realizes the limits of the mind and finds the Lord. This comes to a few through the manifestations of the divine to consciousness; through looking at things with the affirmation of unity as a guide; through the opening of divine disclosures; through inspiration. Those few surpass the whole of creation and reach the level of being servants of God.

And then they serve the rest of creation.

Morals

Ibn 'Arabi says, "No reward that a human being can receive for his achievements can compare with the felicity awarded to whoever shows compassion to humanity." He also says, "God has entrusted animals to men in order to serve them. Treat them gently. When you use them to carry things, do not overload them. When you ride them, do not sit on them proudly." According to Ibn 'Arabi, the essence of morality is compassion.

To help us persevere in treating others with kindness, gentleness, and consideration, he suggests that we be heedful and continuously evaluate, not only our actions, but also our feelings and thoughts.

He says, "May God, who sees everything, open

your inner eye, so that you can see and remember what you have done and thought, felt and said, in your daily life. Remember that you must account for it, and that you will be judged for it on the Day of Reckoning. Do not leave your accounting to that day. This is the time and the place to do it. See yourself, close your accounts. The only way to salvation is to go to the Hereafter clear and clean of all debts. Give heed to the advice of the Messenger of God, who said, 'Make your accounting before it is made for you. Weigh your sins before they are weighed for you.' Weigh your transgressions against your good deeds while you still have time.

"While you are alive, you are like a collector of benefits from God's bounties, which come to you from myriads of hands. What you receive is not really yours. You are like a cashier: you must distribute what you have received, but you are responsible for the accounting of it. If you do not do it today, on the Day of Reckoning no one will come to your aid. You will hear the voice of the Absolute Punisher, Who will say, 'Haven't I sent you messengers, haven't I shown you the right way? Haven't I given you time within the day and within the night to follow My orders, to remember Me and to praise Me? Now:

> Read your book. Your own soul is sufficient as
> a reckoner against you this day.'
> (Surah Bani Isra'il, 14)

"If you wait until the last minute, you will receive no good from your regret. If you cannot see what you are doing, know that the veils covering the eye of your heart are thick, and you are rejected from God's door of mercy. Go and kneel at the sill of that door; shed tears of repen-

63

tance and beg for entrance.

"There are three dangers that may keep you from examining yourself. The first is unconsciousness. The next is the imaginary pleasure you take in the deceptions of your ego. The third is being a slave to your habits."

Ibn 'Arabi practiced the continuous contemplation of his daily life. He mentions that one of his teachers wrote down on a piece of paper everything he did and said during the course of the day. At night he would make an accounting of that day's words and actions. If he had done wrong, he would repent; if he had done right he would offer thanks to God. Ibn 'Arabi himself noted not only what he did and said, but also his thoughts and feelings.

He says, "In whatever state you find yourself, even if you are better than everyone else, ask God for, and work for, a better state. In everything you do, do not forget God."

According to Ibn 'Arabi, contemplation and meditation are a means to protect oneself against all evil. In addition, they inspire patience against adversities.

He believed in the value of all human beings, and in interacting with them with the best of intentions. He says, "Treat everyone equally, whether they are kings or paupers, old or young. Know that humankind is one body, and individuals are its members. A body is not a whole without its parts. The right of the man of knowledge is respect, the right of the ignorant one is advice, the right of the heedless one is to be awakened, the right of the child is compassion and love.

"Treat well those who are dependent upon you: your wives and husbands; your children; the people who work for you; animals in your care; plants in your garden. God has given them into your hands to test you, and you are in His care. Treat the ones in your care as you want the One in whose care you are to treat you. The Messenger of God says, 'All creation are God's dependents. God has left a few of His dependents in your hands. Show love, compassion, delicacy, generosity, and protection toward those who depend on you, and in fact to everyone.'

"Teach your children good behavior with the words of God in His divine book. Secure for them conditions in which they can exercise what you have taught them. From the very beginning, teach them to bear difficulty, to have patience and consideration. Do not place in their hearts the love of the world. Teach them to dislike the things of this world that will render them proud: beautiful clothes, delicacies, luxuries, excess of ambition; because all these will be subtracted from the good due to them in the Hereafter. Let them not become accustomed to good things—yet beware that this, which may seem austere, should not bring forth in you the ugly character of miserliness toward your children.

"In all the good you do, do not expect any return of favors or of thankfulness. When someone causes you pain, do not retaliate by causing them pain. God considers such response as a sin, while He praises the ones who return kindness to those who have hurt them.

"Consider God's orders and fear His justice in everything you do, in everything you say. He is the All-Seeing, the All-Knowing, the Ever-Present. The essence of all religions is to know that although you may not see Him, He sees you. God's orders are only heard and obeyed by the ones who love and fear Him.

"A miser is a coward because he does not have faith in God the Generous. The accursed Devil whispers in his ear that there is no death, he will live a long time, the world is hostile. If he gives what he has, he will be left destitute, dishonored, and alone. He has to look after himself! If this evil imagination captures the heart, it leads to the edge of Hellfire.

"On the other hand, people who give their ears to God will hear Him say:

> *And whoever is saved from the miserliness of his ego, those it is who find salvation.*
>
> (Surah Hashr, 9)

> *Whoever is miserly is miserly to himself.*
>
> (Surah Muhammad, 38)

"Because God will:

> *Destroy their riches and harden their hearts.*
>
> (Surah Yunus, 88)

"God's messenger says, "God has next to Him two angels who pray every morning: 'O Lord, increase your bounties upon the generous, and take away from misers what they have.'"

"The one who gives from his sustenance receives more from God than he gave. The miser, in addition to the sin of miserliness, is guilty of distrusting the Ultimate Sustainer, and depends on his miserable goods over the generosity of his Lord. Therefore spend from what God has given you and do not fear poverty. God will give you what is destined for you, whether you ask for it or not. No one who has been generous has ever perished in destitution.

"If you wish to find God's pleasure and support in finding the truth, avoid being negative and control your temper and your anger. If you cannot stop feeling anger, at least do not show it. If you undertake this, you will disappoint the Devil and please God. That is the beginning of the education of your ego.

"Anger is a result and a sign of an ego out of control—left loose like a wild animal, untied and uncaged. When you hold your temper, it is as if you put a bridle on its head and barriers around it. Then you can begin to tame it so that it obeys and behaves, so that it cannot hurt others than itself—because your ego is still a part of you.

"When you can control your temper, your adversary will be calmed, since you are not reacting to his provocations or responding to his negativity. This is more effective than punishing him. He may be led to see the reality of his acts, to realize what is fair, and to confess his fault.

"Give value to your time. Live in the present moment. Do not live in heedlessness and in imagination and throw your time away. God has prescribed a duty, an act, a worship for your every moment. Know what it is and hasten to do it.

"Use your time first to earn your sustenance lawfully. The Messenger of God says, 'The one who earns his sustenance lawfully through his efforts is beloved of God.' And, 'God likes to see the believer working at his profession.' And, 'God likes the person who has a craft.'

"It is related that one day Hadrat 'Umar, beloved companion of the Prophet, met a group of people who

67

were sitting around lazily doing nothing. He asked them who they were. 'We are of those who put their affairs in the hands of God. We trust in Him,' they replied. 'Indeed, you do not!' he heatedly responded. 'You are nothing but freeloaders, parasites upon other people's efforts. For someone who truly trusts in God first plants the seed in the belly of this earth, then hopes and puts his affairs in the hands of God the Sustainer.'

"First perform the actions that God has given to you as obligations. Next do what He has given you to do through the example of His prophets. Then take on what He has left you as voluntary, lawful, acceptable good deeds. And work to serve the ones who are in need.

"Distance yourselves from the heedless, for they are the slaves of their egos and of the desires of their flesh. They take hearts away from the light of truth and throw them into the dark hole of heedlessness, as they did with their own hearts. If you are forced to be with them in the same time and space, then face them and advise them. If they turn their backs on you, it is because they do not know their fronts from their backs. Be kind to them whether they turn their faces to you or their backs; then they may like you and respect you, and perchance they may become attached to you and follow you on the path of truth.

"Learn proper behavior. It is the means by which an intention becomes a good deed. Therefore it is the greatest capital in the hand of the seeker. The proof is in the words of the one who was brought with the most beautiful character, the last prophet, Muhammad, peace and blessings be upon him, who said, 'I have been sent to perfect good behavior.'"

The Truth of Islam

Ibn 'Arabi says that the name Allah is the proper name of the One and Unique God. It is the name of the essence of God, which contains in itself the beautiful names of all His attributes.

Everything in Islam has generated from the name Allah. It is the cause of the unity of God; the cause of the Holy Qur'an and all other holy books; the cause of worship and prayer. All else is named, but Allah is the Giver of Names. That is why the Messenger of Allah has said, "As long as someone is reciting the Name of Allah, the last day of the world will not come"—because on that day everything named will have ceased to exist. Only Allah, the Namer, will remain.

Ninety-nine beautiful names of Allah have been mentioned in the Holy Qur'an. Some, like "the Ever-Living," "the All-Knowing," are the names of divine attributes. Some, like "the Creator" and "the Sustainer," are the names of divine actions. When one mentions them, one says, "Allah the Ever-Living" and "Allah the Sustainer."

In Islam one declares one's faith by saying *lâ ilaha ill' Allâh*, there is no god but Allah, signifying that all is from Him, and that there is nothing but He. It is not sufficient as a declaration of belief in Him to say *Lâ ilâha ill' al-khâliq*, "there is no God but the Creator"—although Allah is the Creator. One may say that a creative person, a living tree, a sustaining food, carry the manifestations of His attributes in His creation. However, nothing in His creation may be given the name Allah, for He is other than everything He has created and there is none like Him.

In the Muslim declaration of faith, after "There is no god but Allah," it is necessary to bear witness that "Muhammad is His servant and His Messenger."

The Messenger of Allah is a chosen human being, a perfect man. That he is "servant of Allah" shows us the highest level to which any human being can aspire. That he is "Messenger of Allah" is an indication of his closeness to his Lord. He is a guide and an example to humankind whom Allah has sent as a mercy upon the universe, and who Muslims believe will intercede for the faithful on the Day of Judgment. He is human—but as Shaykh 'Abdul-'Aziz Dabbagh, a contemporary of Ibn 'Arabi, says, "If the strength and valor of forty warriors were put into one man who could drag a male lion by the ear, and if that man saw the truth of the Prophet for a single moment, the awe that he felt would tear his lungs from his chest and his soul would leave him."

None can look upon him except the few saints to whom God has given the strength and the ability to see him. Ibn 'Arabi says that he saw him in an ecstatic state, and that he had no shadow—for the source of light has no shadow. God created the divine light, with which everything may be seen and understood, as His first creation. And He placed this divine light in Muhammad, may God's peace and blessings be upon him.

When this light is reflected in the heart of the believer, that heart sees the truth. That person becomes blind to the cognizance of himself, his ego, his flesh, as well as becoming blind to these characteristics in others. It is like when the ladies of ancient Egypt, invited by Zulaykhah to see the beauty of the prophet Joseph, forgot themselves at the sight of him, and cut their fingers while peeling the fruit in their hands.

According to Ibn 'Arabi, the true peace of submission, the truth of Islam, is only possible by passing through that state where one forgets one's self and everything else. The saint Bayazid al-Bistami said: "I was only conscious three times in my life. Once I saw the world. Once I was conscious of the Hereafter. And then one night I saw my Lord, who asked me what I wished, and said He would give it to me. I told Him that I wished for nothing, for He is the Only One."

Thus the truth of Islam cannot be reached without eliminating the worries about this world and the worries about the Hereafter. The ones who can do that are in continuous worship and prayer.

According to Ibn 'Arabi, the way to the truth of Islam is through action and sincerity. The downfall of the ordinary person is to know, but to be unable to act upon that knowledge. For a better person, it is to act upon knowledge but lack sincerity. The danger for the person of higher state is to divulge knowledge without the license of the Lord—for inspired knowledge and the ability to exercise it in sincerity is one of the secrets of the Truth, and can only be shared with others by the permission of the One who gave it.

The confession of faith, "I bear witness that there is no god but Allah and I bear witness that Muhammad is His servant and His Messenger"; daily prayer; fasting during the month of Ramadan; charity; and pilgrimage to Mecca are the five pillars of Islam. Hadrat Ibn 'Arabi adds cleanliness, outer and inner purity, to these five obligations.

He likens Islam to a house with four walls. One

wall is the daily prayer, the other is charity, the third is fasting, the fourth is pilgrimage. There is a double door to this house. Upon one leaf of the door is written "There is no god but Allah", and upon the other, "Muhammad is His servant and His messenger." The roof of that house is cleanliness—purity of body, mind, and soul. In this metaphor we see that if one of the walls is lacking, the house will not stand; and that prayer, fasting, charity, and pilgrimage offer little shelter without purity of being over all.

Ablution, a symbol of cleanliness, is a prerequisite to prayer. According to Ibn 'Arabi, the water used to clean oneself in ablution is a symbol of knowledge. The heart of a believer is alive only if sustained by knowledge.

When there is no water, one can take ritual ablution with sand or earth. Earth too is a symbol of life, for everything alive comes out of it. While taking ablution with water, one washes one's hands and arms to the elbow, one's mouth, one's nose, one's ears, one's face and eyes, one's feet, and also one puts water on one's head. While taking ablution with sand or earth, one does not put earth on one's head, because worship is an attempt to come close to God, while putting earth on one's head is a sign of mourning, of lamentation, when someone beloved is taken away and one is left alone and far off. God says:

> He it is who has made the earth humble, quiet, and submissive to you.
>
> (Surah Mulk, 15)

Earth is the lowest of the four elements. Our need for it to cleanse ourselves is in our need to rid ourselves of the feeling of superiority and arrogance.

Once cleansed, a believer presents himself or herself in front of the Lord five times a day, during the ritual prayers performed at dawn, noon, afternoon, sunset, and night. In the seventeen cycles of obligatory prayer and twenty-three cycles of exemplary prayers, and in other voluntary prayers, we go through certain movements.

First we stand, turning in the direction of the Ka'bah. Wherever believers find themselves on the face of the earth they turn toward Mecca, forming concentric circles. Thus, facing the Ka'bah, we also face each other, symbolically facing the Lord in the hearts of all believers. For God says in a divine tradition, "I do not fit into the heavens and the earth of My creation but I fit into the heart of My believing servant"; and the Prophet says, "The believer is a mirror to the believer."

The prayer starts in a respectful, standing position. When the faithful raise their hands above their shoulders, palms facing forward, and say *Allâhu akbar*, "God is greater than anything He has created," with this gesture they throw the world and their worldly concerns behind them with the backs of their hands. Then they clasp their right hands over their left hands in a respectful position. In this standing position we are to be aware of the human in us, for only the human being is vertical and stands erect. We then recite the opening chapter of the Holy Qur'an:

> *In the name of Allah, the Beneficent, the Merciful.*
> *Praise be to Allah, the Lord of the worlds,*
> *The Beneficent, the Merciful, Master of the Day of Requital.*

Thee do we serve and Thee do we beseech for help.

Guide us on the right path,

The path of those upon whom Thou hast bestowed favors,

Not those upon whom wrath is brought down, nor those who go astray.

(Surah Fatihah, 1-7)

Ibn 'Arabi says that these words are a conversation between the believer and his Lord. When the servant of God says: "In the name of Allah, the Beneficent, the Merciful," the Lord says: "My servant is calling Me." And when he says: "Praise be to Allah, the Lord of the worlds, the Beneficent, the Merciful," the Lord says: "My servant knows Me and he praises Me, for I love him and I overlook his faults." When the believer says: "Master of the Day of Requital," the Lord says: "My servant knows that he will come back to Me, and depends on My justice and forgiveness."

In the center of the chapter is the key verse: "Thee do we serve and Thee do we beseech for help," where the whole of the being, conscious of its exterior actions and expression and of the inner thought and feeling, promises to submit to its Lord's will and beg for His help, declaring that there is nowhere to go but to Him, there is no one from whom to ask for help but from Him. This is the crucial moment in the audience with one's Lord. People who realize this, at this awesome and fearful moment, tremble and shed tears. For the Lord might say: "O tongue, you say that you submit to Me and ask for My help alone, but all the members of that physical body, who have deputized you to talk to Me—your eyes, your mind, your heart—have forgotten Me. Thus, what you say is nothing but a lie." Those who are thus condemned are the people whose minds, eyes, and hearts wander, who look for and see and feel the temptations of this world during prayer.

In the last three verses of the opening chapter of the Holy Qur'an, the Lord speaks to the heart of the servant—for the prayer "Guide us on the right path" calls upon a promise of the Lord, as does "The path of those upon whom Thou hast bestowed favors, not those upon whom wrath is brought down, nor those who go astray."

In the second movement of the ritual prayer, when the believers bow from the waist and repeat thrice *subhâna Rabbîy al-'Azîm* (Glory to my Lord the Most Great), one is conscious of the animal state to which we have been reduced. Most animals roam the earth parallel to the ground. And we plaintively beg our Lord, "Have mercy upon me, O Great One!" Then momentarily we stand up, regaining our human state. With gratitude we throw ourselves into a position of prostration, for realizing our lowliness and the earth from which we are made, we return to the earth.

Then slowly we rise, sitting upon our knees, to remember the Day of Judgment. We turn our heads to the right and then to the left, seeking the help and intercession of those who loved us in this life—our mothers, our fathers, our children—but all in vain; for all will then be concerned with their own fate. The only one immune to the terror of that Day will be the one whom God has sent as His mercy upon the universe, the intercessor for sinners, Muhammad, may God's peace and blessings be upon him.

Before all prayers but one, a formal summons is chanted. The exception is the funeral prayer. And there is no call to prayer that is not followed by worship, except the summons recited into the right ear of a newborn child. The secret is that the call to attend to our departure from this world is issued at the moment we arrive.

The call to prayer consists of reciting four times, "Allah is greater," twice, "I witness that there is no god but Allah," twice, "I witness that Muhammad is the Messenger of Allah," twice, "Come to salvation," twice, "Come to felicity," and again twice, "Allah is greater." Finally, at the end, the reciter says once, "There is no god but Allah."

The reason that these phrases are repeated is that Muslims believe that every human being is born a Muslim—in fact, everything created is created as a Muslim. Some have remembered their original submission to God, while others have not. The first repetition addresses those who realize their state. The second is to remind those who have forgotten.

It is very important that these words be chanted musically and by someone with a most beautiful voice, especially for the congregational prayers in mosques. The Prophet chose Bilal the Abyssinian to perform the call, because his voice was beautiful, although his Arabic was lacking. He said, "When Bilal chants, all the gates of heaven open, up to the throne of God." And when he was asked if that was an honor bestowed on Bilal alone, he answered, "No, this honor belongs to all who call to prayer." In another tradition the Prophet said that the necks of the chanters of the call to prayer are very long—meaning that they will receive blessings as far as their voices reach. He also said that the souls of callers to prayer are together with the souls of martyrs in the Hereafter.

The call to prayer consists of the invitation of God issuing from the lips of a human being. It resembles the revelation of the holy books, which issued from the lips of the prophets. Therefore the real caller to prayer, who invites man to truth and salvation, to peace and felicity, is always the Prophet. As the Lord says in the Holy Qur'an:

> *O our Lord, we have heard the call of one call-*
> *ing to faith "Believe ye in the Lord," and we*
> *have believed.*
>
> (Surah al-'Imran, 193)

Ibn 'Arabi says, "When my Lord made me chant the call to prayer, I saw that each word coming from my lips extended to a distance as far as the eye can see. Then I understood the meaning of the Prophet's words that the necks of the chanters of the call to prayer will be very long, for their Lord's praise for them will be as vast as the area where their voices are heard. The heralds who call the believers to prayer are the best of people, after the prophets, who transmit the truth. The reason that the Prophet of God did not chant the call to prayer himself was because of his compassion for his people. If he himself had called people to prayer, those who couldn't come would have been disobedient to God, and received divine blame for revolting against Him."

Fasting

It is the obligation of every Muslim to fast the whole month of Ramadan, abstaining from eating and drinking and sex from dawn until sunset. During that time it is also important to watch one's emotions, cleansing them from criticism and anger and other negative feelings, as well as protecting oneself from negative impressions, negative thoughts, and negative words. For people at the level of Hadrat Ibn 'Arabi, fasting extends to the whole being. Nothing but God and the godly should enter, not only one's physical being, but also one's heart. Nor should anything leave the being but that which is pure.

Ibn 'Arabi says that the meaning of fasting is self-denial—to deny the evil-commanding ego and the flesh their wishes, which in turn will render the human being pure. No other form of worship or effort to come close to God can equal fasting, for there can be no hypocrisy in it. It is a secret between the Lord and His servant. When one fasts without resentment, sincerely and lovingly, the relation between the fasting servant of God and the Lord becomes selfless, total obedience. One gives up one's will and one's desires, and acts upon the wish of the Lord. That is why God says, "All acts and worship of humankind are for themselves and belong to them. Only fasting is done for Me, and the reward of it is from Me." God also says that the smell of the breath of the one who fasts is sweeter to Him than musk, because what the Lord smells is not the bad odor but the manifestation of His attributes of Patience and Compassion. The one who fasts for God's sake exhales these in each breath.

Charity

Almsgiving is one of the five pillars of Islam. Every year each Muslim is obliged to give one fortieth of his liquid assets to other Muslims in need. As daily prayer and fasting are undertaken for the cleansing of one's soul, alms-giving is the worship proper to one's material belongings. It purifies our possessions and makes them lawful.

As charity is the best of deeds, so stinginess is a grave sin. Hadrat Ibn 'Arabi says, "The one who gives from his sustenance receives more from God than he gave. The miser, in addition to the sin of miserliness, is guilty of distrusting the Ultimate Sustainer, and depends on his miserable goods over the generosity of his Lord. Therefore spend from what God has given you and do not fear poverty. God will give you what is destined for you, whether you ask for it or not. No one who has been generous has ever perished in destitution."

He also relates a story that a saint of the time, mis-understood by the public, was accused of heresy and condemned to be killed. While he was being brought to the place of execution, he passed a baker. He asked the man to give him half a loaf of bread on credit. The baker, having pity on him, gave him the bread. Further ahead on the road there was a beggar. The saint gave the bread to him.

When the procession reached the place of execu-tion, the sentencing judge, following the custom, asked the public gathered there whether they gave their final approval for the execution of the man whom they had declared a heretic and a tyrant. The people cried in unison, "No, this man is a saint, not a heretic! He is the expression of divine justice, not a tyrant!" The judge was shocked to hear this reversal, and had to release him.

The judge asked the saint the reason for the public's favor. "Is your wrath greater, or God's?" the saint inquired. The judge had to admit that God's wrath was greater.

"Is half a loaf of bread larger, or a date?" The judge agreed that half a loaf of bread was larger.

"Haven't you heard the sayings of the Prophet of God?" the saint asked him. "He said, 'Protect yourself from the wrath of God and His punishment by giving to the needy, even if it is half a date.' And also, 'Charity puts out the fire of punishment, and protects from early death.'"

Pilgrimage

The fifth principle of Islam is, once in a lifetime, to perform a pilgrimage to the Ka'bah in the city of Mecca. This is an enactment of the Day of Judgment. One removes all signs of identity and wraps oneself in a shroud; the king and the beggar are made equal. During this stage, one pretends to be dead, selfless. We are forbidden to step on a blade of living green grass, to kill a biting flea, to pull a scab, or even to comb our hair.

Symbolic acts performed during this pilgrimage include circumambulation of the Ka'bah; gathering in millions upon the plains of 'Arafat; and sacrifice of a ram in remembrance of the Prophet Abraham's sacrifice for his son. Ibn 'Arabi says that the literal meaning of *Hajj* (Pilgrimage) in Arabic is the conscious intention to do something at a specific time.

When God addressed the Prophet Abraham

Sanctify My house for those who compass it round or use it for a place of retreat or bow or prostrate themselves [in prayer],

(Surah Baqarah, 125)

He related that house on this planet to Himself. And when He said

The first house appointed for humanity was that at Bakka,

(Surah al-'Imran, 96)

He established it as the first house of worship and assigned it as a symbol of His Throne upon earth. He asked humankind to proceed around it, likening this act to that of the angels who circumambulate His Throne. But the circling of the Ka'bah by people whose words are the sincere confirmation of what is in their hearts, who have cleansed their hearts from the temptations of life on this earth, is a worthier worship than the devotion of the angels circumambulating God's Throne in Heaven.

God built His temple upon three columns, though today it appears to us in the shape of a cube. These three columns are symbolic of the three remembrances of the heart. The one on the corner where the Black Stone is placed represents the divine inspirations. The column in the direction of Yemen represents the angelic characteristics. The third column represents the carnal prompting of human passions. These three supporting columns are guardians; they forbid evil suggestions from entering the house of the Lord. Supported by these three columns, the four sides of the house of God manifest love—although the fourth side of the cube, which faces Iraq, represents the possibility of evil in human beings.

The heart of the believer is the real Ka'bah. It also has the four sides of divine inspirations, angelic attributes, material influences, and diabolic temptations. But the ones who know their Lord have three sides to their

81

hearts. The seductions of evil are absent.

As the daily prayer starts with the declaration "God is greater," so the Pilgrimage begins with the declaration of presence: "O Lord, I am present! I am here now in obedience, ready to receive Your orders! There is none other than You, all praise is due to You, all belongs to You, You have no partners." When the prophet Abraham was ordered to build the Ka'bah, God told him to cry out these words—and in the spiritual realm, the Lord made the souls of all believers hear them. In remembrance, the pilgrims recite this cry.

Male pilgrims wear two pieces of white cloth—one wrapped around the waist, reaching to under the knees, and one to be thrown over the shoulder to cover the torso. Female pilgrims, also dressed in white, may not cover the face. This practice erases all difference of rank and social status, and is a symbol of the shroud.

The white Pilgrimage cloth is not sewn—it is as if not fashioned by human hands. It belongs to God, hiding what is reprehensible or lacking in a human being, protecting from everything that God forbids and from the temptations of the flesh. Like Adam, we carry our sins with us upon the Pilgrimage. But if he had not erred, he would not have descended to our world, where he is honored with being the Deputy of God.

The Black Stone embedded in one corner of the Ka'bah is like the prophet Adam. It also left the Garden pristine and white. It turned black when it entered the earth's atmosphere. Yet the believers kiss it during the Pilgrimage.

At the end of the Pilgrimage, in a place called Mina, each day for three days the pilgrims throw seven stones at the Devil. Humanity knows its Lord through His three aspects: His actions, His attributes, and His existence. The three days represent these three manifestations. The seven stones represent the seven greater sins: pride in one's spiritual state; common arrogance; hypocrisy; envy; anger and negativity; love of property; love of position. Thus the first day one casts these sins out of one's actions, and the second day, out of one's character. On the third day, with the awe of the mystery of God's essence, one casts them from one's being. Finally cleansed, in the place called Mina, which means "Hope" and "Goal," one finishes the Pilgrimage and returns to the world. And then we try to do what is right, and to be what we are meant to be.❧

ON THE TREE OF BEING
SHAJARAT AL-KAWN

IT IS NOT KNOWN when Ibn 'Arabi wrote this short treatise, but there was never a doubt that he wrote it. The main subject of this book, the theme of the Truth of Muhammad, peace and blessings be upon him, is an idea to which he devoted many pages in his last major works, *Fusûs al-Hikam* (Jewels of Wisdom) and *al-Futuhât al-Makkiyyah* (Meccan Gifts to Open the Hearts).

The love of the Prophet to be found here is so intense and expressed in such metaphysical and poetic imagery, written in rhymed prose, that it is impossible to give the same taste of inspiration in translation. And that is another proof that no one else but Ibn 'Arabi could have written these words.

The title given to this work in Arabic is *Shajarat al-kawn*. The literal meaning of *Shajarah* is a tree, with its roots, trunk, branches, leaves, flowers, and fruits. It also means a pedigree, a genealogical tree. *Kawn* in the dictionary is to become, to be, being. Therefore we translated it as The Tree of Being.

This title is for those who only see what is outside and in the language we speak. But for the ones who seek beyond and beneath the physical reality Sayyid Sharif al-Jurjani translates *Shajarah* as Perfect Man and *Kawn* as the Expression of Existence. Thus this book is the description of a perfect human being, Allah's best creation, the Prophet Muhammad, Allah's peace and blessings upon him, written by someone who loved him. Therefore we also chose as a title An Ode to the Perfect Man: The Prophet Muhammad.

The one who wrote these words from beginning to end saw what he saw with the eyes of his heart, wrote what he wrote with the hand of love and in the language of the soul.

And the reader who can leave this world and life of matter somewhat behind, lifting the eyes of his heart to the eyes of his mind, penetrating beyond visual reality, may see the same colors and smell the same perfume of Real Reality that the writer experienced. Who is this perfect man, about whom Allah said:

> *Have We not sent you as a Mercy to all humanity?*
>
> (Surah Anbiya', 107)

And he himself said:

> The one who sees me is looking upon the Truth.

He knew his Lord.

It is an obligation for all people to know their Lord. Perhaps to know one's Lord, one should come to know the one who knows Him, and learn from him. To know such a one, it is not sufficient to know him with whatever strikes the eye—although that is the beginning. This is why we have included a brief description of Prophet Muhammad, peace and blessings be upon him, and the names attributed to him. One has to reach past that, to penetrate into the meaning beyond what is seen. One way to do that is to find the followers of such a perfect man and hear what they say and see what they do in imitation of the one they follow. The principal characteristic of such people is that they give: they give what they have, they give away what they do, they give themselves up, even their lives.

Some such man came home one night and asked his wife if there was anything to eat. When his wife said that there was nothing left, he said, "Thank God and praise Him, our house now is like the home of the Prophet."

And once a beggar came to Ibn 'Arabi's home, begging. He had nothing to give him, so he gave away his home to him.

For such people, this world and what it offers are like an idol.

Once Ibn 'Arabi stood at the gate of a mosque and shouted at the assembly:

The god you worship is under my feet!

They beat him, but later when they dug under where he had stood, they found a treasure of gold.

Once Ibn 'Arabi entered a state of ecstasy and lost himself. This lasted for a long time. When finally he came to himself, he asked what he had done during that time. They said that he had become a humble preacher in a poor, forlorn village.

For him, money and fame did not mean a thing. He was a sultan in the realm of meanings. This he inherited from the one he loved, the one who was the beloved of the Only One: a window opened in this world to look beyond.

And this book describes what can be seen from that window if you open your eyes.❧

THE TREE OF BEING
OF IBN 'ARABI

Seest thou not how Allah sets forth a parable
of a good word as a good tree, whose root is
firm and whose branches are high?

(Surah Ibrahim, 24)

IN THE NAME OF ALLAH, THE BENEFICENT, THE MERCIFUL

ALL PRAISE TO Allah, who is One and Only in His essence and unique in His attributes. Sanctified is He whose regard encompasses everything while transcending all directions. His purity is free and clear of the things seen and imagined.

He goes to places unrestricted by the six directions. He does what He does without acting or doing. He sees everything without looking.

He is far above the meaning of all these things.

His uniqueness does not permit any other to be like Him, nor can anything own or attach itself to Him. His power always reaches its goal and is never spent.

His all-dominating will bears no resemblance to the lowly desires of humankind, nor will His will change with the wishes of His creation; neither will it be in opposition to their solicitations.

His divine attributes, which He manifests upon His creation, neither increase nor decrease when shared with them, for all of His many attributes are but one. He is the cause of all and everything. And when He willed the creation to be, all that He had to do was to say *kun* (Be!), and all that exists came to be.

All that exists was born from the hidden depths of the secret meaning of this word *KUN*. Even all that is hidden from the eye and the mind is but a result of this mysterious sound.

As Allah Most High says:

For to anything We have willed, We but say kun (Be!) and it becomes.

(Surah Nahl, 40)

His word is in itself the deed.

♦

Now I look upon the universe that surrounds us and think how each and every thing came to be and try to solve its coded mysteries, and lo! I see that the whole universe is but a Tree.

A Tree whose light of life came out of a seed shed when Allah said *kun*! The seed of the letter K fertilized with the letter N of *nahnu* (We), created when Allah said:

We it is who have created you.

(Surah Waqi'ah, 57)

Then from these two joined seeds grew two shoots in accordance with Allah's promise:

Verily We have created all things in the way they are determined to be.

(Surah Qamar, 49)

But the root of these two shoots was only a single root.

That root is the will of the Creator, and what it grew into is His power.

Then from the essence of the letter K of the divine word *kun*, two opposing meanings came to be: *kamâliyyah*, perfection, as mentioned by Allah in

> *This day have I perfected your religion and completed My favor to you and chosen for you Islam as your religion,*
>
> (Surah Ma'idah, 3)

and *kufriyyah*, unbelief, as Allah mentioned in

> *So some among them believed and some among them disbelieved.*
>
> (Surah Baqarah, 253)

Likewise from the essence of the letter N emanated the opposing meanings of *nûr al-ma'rifah* (the light of knowledge) and *nakirah* (the darkness of ignorance). Thus when Allah took the creation out of the Hidden Treasure of nonexistence into being, in accordance with its predetermined shape and form, He shed His divine light upon it. Whomever that light fell upon was able to see the Tree of Being that grew from the seed of the divine order *kun* covering the whole universe. And these enlightened ones knew the secret of the K in the word *kuntum* (you are), when Allah said:

> *You are the best community raised up for humanity, you enjoin good and forbid evil and you believe in Allah.*
>
> (Surah al-'Imran, 109)

91

They also penetrated the hidden meaning of the final letter N of *kun* as *nûr* (light). As Allah said:

> *Is he whose heart Allah has opened to Islam so that he follows a light from his Lord (no better than one hard-hearted)?*
>
> (Surah Zumar, 22)

But the ones who hid themselves from the divine light when Allah shed it upon His creation are also obliged to know the hidden meaning of the letters of the word *kun* as Allah pronounced it. Those who kept themselves in the dark will fail to recognize the truth and imagine that the letter K stands for *kufr*, which means the darkness in which they stand, hiding everything from the eye. They will imagine that the letter N stands for *nakirah*, which means ignorance. They become hopeless, and in their hopelessness cannot believe in the existence of their Creator.

So the lot of everything created depends on its share of understanding of the mystery in these two letters, which are the cause of each existence. The proof is in the words of our Prophet, who said:

> Verily Allah created the creation in a realm in total darkness, then shone His divine light upon it. Whoever was lit by that light was enlightened and well guided. And whoever was hidden from that light and was not touched by it was led astray and was lost.
>
> (Ahmad ibn Hanbal)

When our father Adam, the first human being Allah created, opened his eyes—when Allah blew into him his soul from His own soul—he looked at the rest of existence. And he saw it as a circle. Everything was evolving around the circle of Becoming and Being. Actually there are two circles, one of fire and one of wet earth. And he saw that the evolution of the whole universe is a manifestation of the divine order *kun*—the cause, the power, the order of consequent becomings, without fail and forever coming from it.

As no one and nothing can fall out of these revolving circles, nor can any be excluded, it is what they see that counts. Some will see the K as Perfection and strive to be perfect, and some will see it as Unbelief and become disbelievers. Some will find enlightenment in the meaning of the letter N and become wise, and others will find comfort in their heedlessness and think of the letter N as their preference for ignorance over awareness.

None can save themselves from the effect of their faith in what they see as truth. This is determined by the One who created them and what they see, and what they understand from what they see. Everyone is bound to stay within the circumference of the circles on which they revolve. None can be other than what is willed by the One who said Be!, and all became. Everything faces the center of the circle of *kun* and depends on it in all its being.

Then you too look at that Tree of Being, whose branches cover the whole universe. Although every branch, every leaf, every fruit is different, they have all shot up from a single seed, the seed of love named *kun*.

When our father Adam was brought by his Creator to school to learn, to become the human being destined to be the deputy of Allah in the universe, he was first taught all the names of things in existence.

Then in awe he faced the word *kun*, the divine order Be, the cause of all being. What did it mean? He sought the intention of the One who brought all this into being and saw that the first letter K related to the word *kanziyyah* (the Hidden Treasure), when Allah said:

> I was a hidden treasure and I loved to be known, and I created the creation so that I would be known.

And in the last letter N he saw the identity of the Creator, when He said *anâ Allâh* (I am Allah)

> *Surely I am Allah, there is no god but I, so serve Me...*
>
> (Surah Ta Ha, 14)

Then one after another it was revealed to him that the K of the *kanziyyah* indicated the gifts of Allah upon him and his progeny in the word *karam* (generosity) of his Lord, as promised in His words:

> *And surely We have honored the children of Adam and We carry them on land and sea, and We provide them with good things, and We have made them to excel highly above most of those whom We have created.*
>
> (Surah Bani Isra'il, 70)

And again, the K meant to Adam *kuntiyyah* (becoming, from "I become") in Allah's promise, which He said:

94

When My faithful servant comes close to Me
with extra devotions, he loves Me and I love
him; and when I love him, I become his eyes
with which he sees, I become his ears with
which he hears, I become his hands with
which he holds…

And he understood that the letter N at *anâ Allâh*
was meant to shed the *nûr*, the divine light, upon him and
those like him, as Allah said:

*Is he who was lifeless, then We raised him to life
and made him a light by which he walks
among people, like him whose likeness is that
of one in darkness whence he cannot come
forth?*

(Surah An'am, 122)

And the N of *kun* pointed to the N in the word
ni'mah, bounties of Allah, in Allah's words:

*He gives you of all you ask of Him. And if you
try to count Allah's bounties, you will not be
able to count them.*

(Surah Ibrahim, 34)

These are some of the things that our father Adam
learned about the divine word *kun* in Allah's school in
Paradise—not all. We have only mentioned less than the
least. More will be told later.

Now the accursed Devil went to the same school of
instruction in Paradise, and for forty thousand years he
studied, examining the secrets in the letters of the word
kun. But the Divine Teacher willed that he should depend

95

on his own powers and feel confident and able to do things by himself. So when he examined the meaning of the letter K he associated it with his dependence only upon himself and on his unbelief (*kufr*) in any other power but his own, as told by His Lord:

> *He disdainfully refused to obey Allah and became proud...*
>
> (Surah Baqarah, 34)

And he saw in the letter N his own fiery nature in the word *nâr* (fire), and said:

> *I am better than Adam: You have created me of fire, while You created him of earth.*
>
> (Surah A'raf, 12)

So the *kufr* which the Devil identified with in the letter K pushed him to the *nâr* which he saw in the letter N, and his destiny and the destiny of the likes of him was set:

> *So they were hurled into Hellfire*
>
> (Surah Shura, 94)

When our father Adam looked at the Tree of Being, in the splendor of the many kinds of flowers and fruits on its many lofty branches, he left them all but held onto the branch of

> *Surely I am Allah, there is no god but I...*
>
> (Surah Ta Ha, 14)

He knew that it was the only thing that is sure and unalterable. So he took refuge in the security of solitude in the oneness of his Lord. While in that state of unison a soundless and wordless message came, both to him and to our mother Eve:

> *O Adam, dwell you and your wife in the garden and eat from whence you desire, but go not near this tree.*
>
> (Surah A'raf, 19)

But the accursed Devil would not leave them be. He was holding onto the branch of false imagination, and he willed to fool them. Indeed he succeeded, and made Adam and Eve eat from the forbidden tree. And they disobeyed their Lord's order:

> *…go not near this tree.*

Yet they were aware of what they did wrong. So when they slipped down from their peace of unison with their Lord, they caught onto the branch of repentance and said:

> *Our Lord we have wronged ourselves; and if You forgive us not nor have mercy on us, we shall certainly be of the losers.*
>
> (Surah A'raf, 23)

And holding onto that branch, which saved them, they received words in the form of sweet fruits growing on it:

> *Then Adam received words from his Lord and He turned to him mercifully; surely He is Oft-returning to mercy, Most Merciful.*
>
> (Surah Baqarah, 37)

There is a day that is called The Day of Witnessing, and on that day under the eyes of the whole, witnessing, every soul will hear its Lord ask:

Am I not your Lord?

(Surah A'raf, 172)

and they will all say:

Yes; we bear witness.

(Surah A'raf, 172)

But they will bear witness to the extent of what they saw and knew, although they all answered in agreement, saying Yes; verily. Those who have seen the divine beauty of their Lord's Essence will say:

Nothing is like Him.

(Surah Shura, 11)

Those who have seen the beauty of His divine attributes will say:

He is Allah, beside whom there is no god—the Owner of All, the All-Holy, the Granter of Peace, Protector of All, the Mighty, the Supreme, the Possessor of All Greatness. Glory be to Allah over the partners they ascribe. He is Allah, the Creator, the Evolver, the Fashioner of Everything. His are the most Beautiful Names. Whatever is in the Heavens and the Earth declares His glory, and He is the Mighty, the Wise.

(Surah Hashr, 23-24)

Those who have only thought of Allah in relation to the beauty of the things He has created will all imagine their Lord differently, in accordance with their impressions of the things they see. Some will put God within a limited frame of space and time. Some will even think that He does not exist. And some will make a shape out of stone and think it to be He. Woe to those whose destiny is this! And they say:

> ...nothing will afflict us save that which Allah
> has ordained for us.
>
> (Surah Tawbah, 51)

Indeed their lot is also included among everything that happened when the Creator pronounced the word *kun* and that word became the center of the whole created universe, revolving around it; and when from that center grew the Tree of Being, the word *kun* being the seed from which it grew.

If one wanted to visualize all there is as a whole— everything that came into existence and what caused them all to be, and their doings and their sayings, and their lives, and their states, and their interactions—what better similitude is there for seeing this than a tree, the Tree of Being? A tree that contains all that happens in the universe, generating from a single divine seed, made out of the voice of our Lord, who said *kun*!

As that Tree grows, everything appears on it. Things become more, things become less, some things are seen, and others are hidden: faith and faithlessness, the fruits of good deeds, states of purity, sounds and meanings of beautiful words, right wishes and hopes, good character and gentle behavior, sensitivity to beauty and the knowledge of reality are some of its leaves and flowers. The levels the pious reach, the approval the righteous receive, the closeness to their Lord of the ones who know their Lord, the annihilating fire of love of the lovers of Allah—these are some of the fruits of the Tree of Being.

First, three shoots grew from the sacred seed of that Tree. One of those shoots bent to the right and grew in that direction. That will bear the fruits of

> ...those on the right hand; how happy are
> those on the right hand!
>> (Surah Waqi'ah, 27)

Another shoot grew towards the left

> ...and those on the left hand; how wretched
> are those on the left hand!
>> (Surah Waqi'ah, 41)

The third shoot grew tall, going upwards, and

> the foremost are the foremost, these are drawn
> nigh to Allah.
>> (Surah Waqi'ah, 10-11)

And the Tree of Being grew, reaching the far heavens. Its lower branches became the worlds of matter; its higher branches became the worlds of ideas and the meanings of things. The world we live in is only the bark of that Tree; its inner core is where the spirit resides. And the life-giving sap running in its veins, the power making it grow and give flowers and fruits is the realm of the uncreated, omnipotent universe, the *jabarût*, where the secret of the word *kun* is hidden. That is the realm where the essence is kept. What we see are the attributes and the names, which act as its deputies.

The Tree of Being is protected within a wall that surrounds it on its right and on its left, in front of it and in back of it, above it and beneath it. The worst of the worst is at its lowest limit; the best of the best is at its highest level. Around this blessed Tree, as far as the eye can see, are the stars in the heavens, the things around us, the names by which they are called, the ways they behave, and what they do to each other. The seven heavens are like its leaves, which give shade; the stars are like its flowers. The night and the day are like two covers, one of them black and the other white, with which the Tree is covered twice a day. When the black veil covers it, it disappears from sight. When it is covered with white, it gives light to the eyes, which wish to see the beautiful sight.

The Divine Throne of Power is where the Tree of Being receives all it needs. It is a bottomless treasure that sustains it; an inexhaustible powerhouse that protects it. That is where the angels, the servants of the Tree of Being, those who take care of it, dwell.

> *And you see the angels going about the Throne of Power, glorifying their Lord...*
>
> (Surah Zumar, 75)

So the angels face the Throne of Power and receive whatever is needed from it. Wherever they are, they are flying around it and pointing to it.

Whenever something fails in the divine harmony of the Tree of Being, whenever an unexpected thing happens, the angels raise their hands toward the Throne, begging for forgiveness for their failure in their service and seeking the help of the Maker of the Tree, for there is

101

no one else to turn to. And the One who made that Tree is neither here nor there, but everywhere. He can neither be seen nor known—yet everything known, while not He, is from Him. The Divine Throne is a manifestation of His power, not where He resides.

Yet if the Throne were not a direction toward which the angels might face when they are serving the Tree of Being in His name and for His sake, they would not have known where to turn to ask for help and to render their obedience, and they would have gone astray and been lost. So the Creator of all created the Divine Throne, not as a place for His Essence to dwell, but as a source of power for His creation to turn to, to receive what it needs.

He created the creation, not that He had any need for it, but to have His attributes seen and His beautiful names known.

One of His names is the Forgiving One: that is why He created the ones who will receive His forgiveness. One of His names is the Compassionate One: that is why He created the ones who will need His compassion. One of His names is the Generous One. That is why He created the ones in need and their needs: to manifest His generosity upon them.

All the branches of this Tree bear different fruits. Thus each created being is different from each other created being, and so are what they do and what they serve. There are as many differences in the creation as the number of the attributes of the One who created it. Thus each and every one of His beautiful names and His attributes is materialized and manifested.

He created the sinners, and the wrongs they did, and their repentance, and so manifested His forgiveness.

He created the good and their deeds, and unfolded His mercy upon them. He created His obedient servants and poured His favors upon them. He manifested His justice upon the disobedient and His wrath upon the unfaithful.

Yet the manifestation of His attributes in His creation bears no resemblance to Him nor is attached to Him, is not even close to Him; all is from Him, but is not He. He existed always, when nothing existed. And when He created the universe, He neither grew nor gained anything. If all should disappear, He will lose nothing. He is now as He always was and forever will be. Although He is not joined with His manifestation in the attributes of the things He has created, neither is He separated from the things that came from Him. For union and separation are acts that belong to creatures that come into being, not to the Eternally Existent One, who is unique and alone. Union and separation involve movement toward and away from one another. This movement involves change of space and time and state, and even disappearance. All these are attributes of imperfection, while the Creator of All is one, unique, eternal, and perfect.

♦

Allah created a Hidden Tablet and a Pen to write the constitution of His universal kingdom, which contains all His decisions, decrees, and ordinances about things created, things to be created, things to die and disappear; and the sustenance, rewards, and punishments that each deserves and will receive.

Then Allah marked the limit beyond which neither His creatures nor their knowledge may ever reach by planting a Lotus Tree above the Seventh Heaven

...the farthest Lotus Tree.

(Surah Najm, 14)

All that comes from Allah, and all that is sent up from below, stops there.

The Lotus Tree is the uppermost branch of the Tree of Being. Under its shade are the angels who transmit what comes from Allah to those below, and send up to Him whatever reaches them from His creatures below. On that branch a copy of what is written in the Hidden Tablet hangs. Whatever occurs on the Tree of Being cannot reach beyond that point. That which grows, that which is ripe, that which rots stays below it.

Everything in creation has a station, a limited place that is known, a shape that is prescribed. All have a destiny in the way they lead their lives, for

> *there is none of us but has an assigned place.*
>
> (Surah Saffat, 164)

None of the fruits of the Tree of Being can rise above its assigned place. Whether it is beautiful or ugly, great or insignificant, royal or humble, rare or common, the destiny of each is written in the copy of the Hidden Tablet hanging on that branch.

> *And the book is placed...what book is this! It leaves out neither a small thing, nor a great one, but numbers them all...*
>
> (Surah Kahf, 49)

Nothing is unaccounted for which grows on that Tree, nor is anything cast away. So the Lord ordained that the fruits of that Tree be stored in two different places, and called them Paradise and Hell. The pure, unblemished, beautiful fruits are stored in Paradise above:

> *Surely the record of the righteous is in the*
> *highest places*
>
> (Surah Mutaffifîn, 18)

And the rotten fruits are stored in the Hell below:

> *Surely the record of the wicked is in the prison*
> *of hell.*
>
> (Surah Mutaffifîn, 7)

Paradise is on the right side of the mountain where the Lord spoke to Moses, where the blessed

> *ones on the right hand*

reside.
And Hell is by

> *...the tree of Zaqqûm, which is the food of the*
> *sinful*
>
> (Surah Dukhan, 43-44)

> *...the tree cursed in the Qur'an*
>
> (Surah Bani Isra'il, 60)

where the wretched

> *ones on the left...*
> *reside.*

This world of ours, in which we reside, is a place where the Lord exhibits the choice flowers of the Tree of Being, each and every one shown only for awhile. And He has made the next world, the Hereafter, to store its fruits to be preserved eternally. The wall, the limit to protect this Tree of Being, surrounds all of it, as

> *He surely encompasses everything.*
>
> (Surah Fussilat, 54)

And He put a circle around it, so that nothing else but His will could touch it.

> *Surely Allah decides whatever He pleases*
> (Surah Zariyat, 1)
> *...and does whatever He wills.*
> (Surah al-'Imran, 39)

When the truth of that tree was firmly rooted and its branches were fully formed, it grew in all directions, for

> *to your Lord is the goal of it.*
> (Surah Nazi'at, 44)

It grew till its front reached its back and its end reached its beginning. Does not Allah say:

> *For to anything that We willed, We but say Be (kun) and it becomes (yakûn).*
> (Surah Nahl, 40)

So it began by the divine order Be, and finished by Becoming. No matter what multitude of branches it has, it has only one root, growing from a single seed named *kun*.

Thus, if you truly look and seek the reality, you will see that everything is interconnected and really one. The celestial tree called *Tûbâ* growing in Paradise is connected by its roots to the poisonous tree of *Zaqqûm* growing in Hell. The coolness of the gentle celestial breeze of *Qatb* mingles with the hellish heat of the infernal wind of *Simûm*. The refreshing shade of the final station in Heaven for the best of us is connected with the fuming black mist of Hell where the worst of us will go.

106

So all receive what is destined for them from the same source. Some drink from the cup that is best for them; some drink from the cup that should be sealed closed for them. And there are those who are forbidden to drink at all.

When the ones who have been brought into existence started giving birth to new beings coming forth from nothingness, Allah blew upon them His Breath of Power, fed them with the nourishment of His wisdom, and washed them with rain from the clouds of His will. When all these blessings touched the Tree of Being, its branches bore the predestined fruits. Then according to their nature, both health and sickness befell them.

The universe grew from the two consonants of the Divine word *kun.* One begets light and the other, darkness. All good comes from that light and all harm comes from that light, so only good comes from it, and

> *they do not disobey Allah in that which He commands them, but do as they are commanded.*
>
> (Surah Tahrim, 6)

The Devil and his followers are born in the darkness, and only evil comes from them. As for Adam and his children, the clay from which they are made is a mixture of both light and darkness. There are both good and evil in their nature, and in their actions lie things both beneficial and harmful. In their lives they might choose to come close to their Lord or to deny Him, seeking their origin or losing it; they are the way they are depending on which part of their nature dominates. Thus if the light in their essence is dominant, their spirit becomes the master of their flesh;

in the eye of their Lord they become better than the angels; their spirit soars above the heavens. But if their flesh crushes their spirit and the darkness of their nature puts out the light in their being, then they are reduced below the level of animals, one step above the accursed Devil.

When Allah took a handful of earth that His word *kun* contained and made it into the shape of Adam, He stroked its back to separate that which was clean from that which was soiled. So the good people of the right hand fell to the right side, and the evil people of the left hand fell to the left side. Not a single one of Adam's children is able to pass to the side other than the one the Lord willed. And no one can oppose the will of Allah, nor can any ask why.

♦

When the One who was planting the Tree of Being first squeezed the quintessence out of its seed, He churned it till its cream rose to the surface, than passed it many times through a sieve to filter any dregs that might have been in it. When it became purer than the purest, He shone upon it the light of wisdom. It became alive, and He dipped it into His ocean of mercy so that the whole creation could share its blessings. Then from it He created the light of our Prophet Muhammad, may Allah's peace and blessings be upon him. He decorated this light with lights from the highest angelic realm to enhance its beauty and brightness. This light is the origin—the source of all and everything that comes into being.

So our master Muhammad, peace and blessings be upon him, was the first among Allah's chosen and the last to appear as a prophet among human beings to bring them the good news of felicity in this world, to put the crown of faith on their heads, and to be their intercessor on the Day of Judgment. His origin is kept inscribed in the sacred book of Allah as His Beloved. He lives in the paradise of closeness to his Lord. His spirit is with his Maker, but it is hidden under his resemblance to other men. He was sent as Allah's mercy upon the universe, which the Creator created for his sake. If it were not for him, the universe wouldn't be there.

When the Creator created this universe, for which He had no need, He meant to manifest His power over it, and the perfection of His wisdom, so that life comes forth from earth and water. Did He say about anything else that He brought into life

> *I am going to place it as a ruler in the universe.*
>
> (Surah Baqarah, 30)

Only human beings out of the whole creation were told

> *He it is who has made you His successors in the land.*
>
> (Surah An'am, 166)

So the purpose of the creation of humanity and the honor bestowed upon humankind is to bring forth among them the first-created light of Muhammad in human form. He is the realization of the K in the divine word *kun* in the word *kanz* (Hidden Treasure), when Allah said:

I was a hidden treasure and I loved to be

109

known, and I created the creation so that I would be known.

So then, what is proper for the created is to know their Creator. And the One who loves to be known is in the heart of His Beloved, whose light was His first creation, and to whom He has shown Himself on the night of his ascension. With faith and trust in him, people see by his light and know their Lord as he saw Him, and all praise him. May Allah's peace and blessings be upon our master Muhammad!

Thus Allah created His beloved, Muhammad, from the seed of the divine order *kun*:

> *...like a seed which puts forth its roots*
>
> (Surah Fath, 29)

and strengthened him by his blessed companions with firm hearts, as the tree is

> *...strengthened, so it becomes stout and stands firmly on its trunk*
>
> (Surah Fath, 29)

under his Lord's eyes and with His help.

Now when this mighty branch of Muhammad appeared on the Tree of Being, and its foliage reached far and wide, the clouds of acceptance were attracted by it and poured rain upon the Tree of Being. And all that which was created, and men and *jinn*, rejoiced, and breathed the perfume of its budding flowers.

The day Muhammad, peace and blessings be upon him, was born, the false gods made by human hands fell on their faces and were gone, and religions of old were abrogated. Allah sent down the Qur'an to confirm his presence, and the Tree of Being burst into flowers and fruits of joy. Even the people of the left hand, on the far left of the Tree, whose natures lead them to evil, will hear when the winds of Allah's message reach their way:

> *We have not sent you save as a mercy to the whole creation*
>
> (Surah Anbiya', 107)

and hope. But this promise is only for

> *...those for whom good has already gone forth from Allah.*
>
> (Surah Anbiya', 101)

So those who are destined to be good are the ones who will smell the perfume of the promised garden in the sweet breeze coming from the Prophet, and move toward him with love. But for the disgraced on the left hand, heedless in both body and soul, the same gentle breeze will turn into a hurricane of divine wrath and blow them away. They saw themselves flourishing: how much worse is the shock of finding themselves withered and dried up, the joy on their faces turned to an ugly grimace, and the hope of their riches turned into poverty and despair!

There is a secret of that branch of Muhammad on the Tree of Being: it came to be when it was grafted from the tree of free existence, and from the spirit of that graft came Muhammad's shining pearl of spirit.

> *O Prophet, We have sent you as a witness and a bearer of good tidings, and as a warner, one who summons to Allah by His permission; and as a clear, shining sun.*
>
> (Surah Ahzab, 45-46)

111

So he is the sun, shedding light upon the dark universe, and the soul in the body of existence, responding to Allah's order when He addressed the heavens and the earth:

Come you two, willingly or unwillingly. They both said: we come willingly.

(Surah Fussilat, 11)

The Ka'bah on earth and the Ka'bah above it in the heavens also heard and obeyed, and came down and became the center of true faith on earth.

When Allah sent His angels to bring a handful of earth from this world to fashion the form of Adam, they brought earth from all climes, some black, some red, and some white clay, without minding if it was better or worse. But when his Lord was going to fashion the form of our master Muhammad, peace and blessings be upon him, the earth was picked from the site of Holy Ka'bah, the center of true faith in Allah. In the creation of all other human beings Allah mixed that clay with the clay of Adam and kneaded it till it became like bread dough: thus He made humankind. If the children of Adam did not have a trace of our master the Beloved of Allah in them, on the Day of Witnessing none would have been able to say:

Yes, we bear witness

(Surah A'raf, 172)

when Allah asked:

Am I not your Lord?

(Surah A'raf, 172)

It is due to this mystery in the creation of Adam that our master, the Messenger of Allah, said:

> I was a prophet when Adam was still between water and earth. (Tirmidhi)

So the good nature and the blessing in everybody and everything that has come into being is by the grace of the traces of Muhammad, peace and blessings be upon him, in them. And on that day when every part of each person will be a witness against them, and the Divine Judge asks:

> *Am I not your Lord?*

they will say

> *Yes, we bear witness.*

That drop from the clay of their Prophet's body will dominate their bodies, their lives, their tongues, if their predetermined natures enable them to hold and retain it. So it grows in them, and when they are born into this world, it becomes their shape and form, their attributes and actions. Then their beautiful spirit shines through the darkness of flesh. When they are summoned by their Lord, they are able to say in total obedience:

> *I am here and now, my Lord; I am at your service*

But the ones whose clay is spoiled will not be able to keep this drop from the clay of Muhammad, nor will it grow in them. At first they will also answer "Yes," affirming their Lord, but they will soon forget. So the blessed drop will rot in the corrupt soil in the nature of the evil one, and fall out. It is as if one entrusts something valuable to someone corrupt and then takes it back because that person is not worthy to guard it. Like this, at the beginning faith is also in the hearts of unbelievers, yet only in the hearts of believers does it remain. As the Prophet said:

> Every child is born naturally as a Muslim, but his environment makes him into a Jew or a Christian or a magian. (Bukhari, Tirmidhi, Jami')

In the beginning, all people said "Yes" when they were asked, "Am I not your Lord?" because at first every part of their being contained the traces of the Prophet's clay. This was the will of their Lord. But only those who acted upon their Lord's will and worked hard to keep this gift were able to keep it. Since Allah has decreed that those chosen will keep it, no force in the world can appropriate it.

◆

The way the Tree of Being grows and bears flowers and fruits is the manifestation of thoughts, wishes, and hopes—pleasure taken in things beautiful, secret intentions, shedding tears for past faults, efforts in doing good deeds. It is the purification of the self, human hearts as wide and peaceful as green fields. It is the discovery of hidden mysteries—the inner eye viewing the inner reality, the mind grasping the true meaning of sacred words, the flowers of wisdom blossoming, the blessing of knowing the truth ascending far above, over everything, where the sweet breezes of felicity caress one's cheeks. It is the praised achievements of the ones who know the origin of things, and the state in which the trace of the Prophet exists; the levels reached by the righteous, the divine secrets shared by the ones close to their Lord, and the unseen seen by the ones who drown in the ocean of love. But what is all this compared to what is in the heart of Allah's Beloved, the first, the last, and the best of His creation, Hadrat Muhammad Mustafa? All these ornaments on the Tree of Being are but the fruits of the graft from the branch of Muhammad, a little beam from his light, a cup from his fountain in Paradise to quench the thirst of all the faithful, a bite out of his feast of beneficence, a single word learned in his school of guidance.

As his Lord said about him

We have not sent you save as a mercy upon the universe

(Surah Anbiya', 107)

so His mercy covers everything.

Allah celebrates everywhere in the wide universe the glory of Muhammad. Days and nights labor only for him. Borders are set around lands where his mission will flourish and where his name is exalted, the secrets and decrees brought by him respected, and the truth offered by him, accepted. All hold onto the words of Allah coming from his blessed lips as a drowning person holds onto a life-saving cord thrown to him. All the prophets prior to him follow his mission, and Allah's ordinances for the good of all humanity revealed to him are the law both for those who follow him and for those who turn their backs. He is the Last Prophet and the Seal of Prophethood until the end of time. Allah's words in the Qur'an, revealed to him, contain all that He sent prior to it. They will not be changed and are valid until the end of time.

So whoever takes refuge in him is safe and secure, and whoever follows his path will be led away from evil and into salvation.

When Adam sinned and was chased from the Garden and sent to this world of exile, he was pardoned only when he begged for forgiveness in the name of Muhammad.

By the grace that Muhammad would come from the lineage of Abraham, the fire into which Abraham was thrown turned into a rose garden.

And when Abraham was ordered to sacrifice his son, Ishmael was redeemed in the name of Muhammad.

♦

Allah said about the relation to Muhammad of the chosen who are

> *the foremost, those who are drawn nigh to Allah*
>
> (Surah Waqi'ah, 10-11)

who are the fruits of the shoot that grew straight up in the Tree of Being:

> *Muhammad is the Messenger of Allah, and those with him are firm at heart against the disbelievers and compassionate among themselves. You see them bowing down, prostrating themselves, seeking Allah's grace and pleasure. Their marks are on their faces in consequence of prostration. That is their description in the Torah and the Gospel—like*

116

seed produces its sprout, then strengthens it, so it becomes stout and stands firmly on its stem... Allah has promised such of them as believe and do good, forgiveness and a great reward.

(Surah Fath, 29)

And He said about the blessed ones of the right hand, the fruits of the shoot that bent to the right when it sprouted from the seed of *kun*:

...a people whom He loves and who love Him, humble toward believers, mighty against the disbelievers, striving hard in Allah's way and not fearing the censure of any censurer. This is Allah's grace—He gives it to whom He pleases. And Allah is Ample-Giving, All-Knowing.

(Surah Ma'idah, 54)

And Allah said about the unfortunate creatures of the left hand, rotten fruits of the shoot that bent left when it sprouted from the same seed:

Allah would not chastise them while Muhammad is with them; nor would Allah chastise them while they seek forgiveness.

(Surah Anfal, 33)

Thus the Lord covered the whole world with His mercy, which is Muhammad, peace and blessings be upon him, and perfected His religion, which is Islam. His message to humanity is finalized in the Qur'an. He created the creation for the sake of Muhammad, and in his shape. The shape of Adam and his children is creat-

117

ed in the form of the name of Muhammad. The round-
ness of their heads comes from the Arabic letter M. The
two arms hanging down from each side are each in the
form of the letter H. The belly is like the second M in
the writing of Muhammad, and the legs spread apart is
from the Arabic letter D. Thus the Lord wrote the name
of His beloved in the shape of humankind.

Now think how the rest of the creation is but a
duplicate of his body and soul. For there is not a single
universe, but two. One is the universe of matter and the
other is the spiritual universe; the visible and the invisible
worlds. Muhammad's body became the model for the visible world, and the spiritual realms were inspired by his
blessed soul. So the density and the weight of things in
this lower world are as the weight of his material existence among us. And the fine beauty and grace of the
celestial, spiritual world are like his divine soul. All the
mountains in the world holding the earth in place are like
his bones holding up his blessed body, and all the waters
in this world, some still, some flowing, some sweet, some
bitter, are like the blood flowing in his veins, or standing
at his joints, and like the secretions of the body: sweet like
his saliva, which sweetens what is drunk or eaten; or salty
like the tears that moisten and protect the eye; or bitter
like the wax in the ear, which repels flies and insects.

The surface of this earth is like his blessed body. The
fertile lands are like places where hair grows; the barren
lands are like places where there is none. And the great
lakes from which flow rivers, which divide into streams,
watering lands for the benefit of humanity, are like his
heart that pumps blood into arteries and small veins,
reaching every part of his blessed body, keeping it alive.

The skies above are the visible symbol of the spiritual realms we cannot see. There the Lord has placed a sun and a moon shedding light upon mankind:

See you not, how Allah has created the seven heavens alike, and made the moon therein a light and made the sun a lamp?

(Surah Nuh, 15-16)

In the same manner, He has placed the soul in the body to make it luminous, to find the right path in life. And at the end, when it departs, the corpse is left in the dark, just as the night comes upon the earth when the sun departs.

The human mind is like the moon: at certain times dimmer, and at certain times brighter. When it first appears it is a dim, thin crescent, like the mind of a child. Then it grows into a full moon, and then it is reduced to none. Thus humanity gain their full powers at the age of forty in the middle of life. Then they decline.

Allah has created five planets in the skies:

Every soul will know what it has prepared. Nay, I call to witness the stars, running their course and setting.

(Surah Takwir, 14-16)

Saturn, Jupiter, Mars, Venus, and Mercury are like the five senses of seeing, hearing, touching, smelling, and tasting in man, which the Lord will call as our witnesses on the Day of Judgment.

Then far above, in heavens unseen, the Lord has set a Throne and a Pedestal:

119

> *He created the heavens and the earth and
> what is between them in six periods, and He is
> established on the Throne of Power*
>
> (Surah Sajdah, 4)

where

> *He knows that which goes down into the earth
> and that which comes forth out of it, and that
> which comes down from heaven and that
> which goes up to it. And He is with you wher-
> ever you are. And Allah sees all that you do.*
>
> (Surah Hadid, 4)

He set the Throne of Power as a direction toward which the hearts of the believers should turn, a sign toward which hands should be lifted in prayer. It is neither where His essence is nor where His attributes are established. He says:

> *The All-Merciful is established on the Throne
> of Power.*
>
> (Surah Ta Ha, 5)

The Merciful One is but one of His divine attributes and exists in praise of Him, and is indeed a manifestation of His essence, which is also manifest in His creation. While His essence is uncreated, the Throne of Power is a created thing. It is not attached to Him, nor even comes close to Him; certainly He does not sit on it, nor need it.

As for the Pedestal, it is a gate to His secrets and a curtain over His divine light, by which

He knows what is before them and what is behind them. And they encompass nothing of His knowledge except what He pleases. His Pedestal extends over the heavens and the earth, and the preservation of them both tires Him not. And He is the Most High, the Tremendous.

(Surah Baqarah, 255)

He has made the breast of the human being as a model of His Pedestal, where all knowledge enters and comes out to be used. It is like a courtyard set before two gates: one to the heart and the other to man's evil-commanding self. So all the good that enters the heart and all the mischief that penetrates the self, which come out as good and evil acts, generate from the breast, as Allah says:

And that which is in the breasts is made manifest.

(Surah 'Adiyat, 10)

He has made the human heart as a model of His Throne of Power in the heavens. His Throne in the heavens is known to exist, but His throne in the heart was made to be His home. The Throne in the heavens does not contain Him, nor is He seated upon it; He does not even touch it. Yet His throne in the human heart is always in His sight; it is where He reveals and manifests Himself, and He pours His blessings upon it from the heavens. Allah says:

I do not fit into the heavens and earths that I created, but I fit into the loving heart of My faithful servant.

(Hadith Qudsi)

♦

Then Allah created Paradise and Hell for the life of the Hereafter. He decorated His Paradise with beauty and prepared it for the felicity and peace of the ones he loves. He turned Hell into an image of His wrath for the punishment of the evil ones. Paradise is a reflection of all the good deeds done, and Hell is shaped in the image of all the disasters caused by its inhabitants.

Likewise Paradise in this life, the treasure of all good is in that black dot inside the heart—the heart of the heart of His faithful servant. That is where He reveals Himself, where revelations and divine inspirations descend, where sincere supplications come forth; it is the source of divine light showing the right way.

And Hell is locked in man's evil-commanding self: the dark deep will of dirty deeds. In its total darkness one is fooled by one's imagination, seen as reality, where the evil gaze on flames of sin.

♦

Then Allah created the Hidden Tablet and the Pen to write, determining all beings that are, that were, and that will be until the end of time. And He created the angels to do what He bids them to do. They hear from their Lord concerning creation, annihilation, life, death, confirmation, alteration, diminution, augmentation; all that has happened, is happening, and will happen in the whole creation.

The human tongue is like the Pen, and the human breast is like the Hidden Tablet. Whatever is said is written in the breast as memory to be remembered, and whatever the heart desires is raised to the tongue, which interprets it inwardly. Allah chose the senses as the messengers of the heart. The ear is the heart's spy, listening to secrets. The eye is in the heart's employ as a watchman and a guard. The tongue is given the duty of being the heart's interpreter, through which the heart speaks in words that people may understand.

♦

And the Lord created a certain property in the human being as a proof of His Lordship and the truth of the prophethood of Muhammad, peace and blessings be upon him. That is the soul. The human being, whom He created as the epitome of the universe, is a world; a kingdom in himself. This kingdom needs a king to rule it, so Allah created the soul to rule it. This ruler is alone, he is hidden from the eye: no one knows where he is. Not a hair moves on the body without the soul knowing it. The soul made it move in the first place, and nothing is seen or felt or done save by the soul.

Now as the human kingdom, the epitome of the universes seen and unseen, needs the soul as its king, so the rest of the creation is also in need of a ruler with qualities like those of the human soul: one and unique, hidden from the eye, unlike anything known or unknowable; one who knows everything happening in his kingdom and causes all that happens, who is in and out with everything without being with them; invisible, untouchable, beyond reach, all-powerful ... and even all these bear no relation to Him:

> *Nothing is like Him: and He is*
> *All-Hearing and All-Seeing.*

(Surah Shura, 11)

♦

Allah sent upon His creation two deputies. One was present among them, like them. The other was hidden from the eye, a spirit. The apparent one is Muhammad, peace and blessings be upon him, the Messenger of Allah. The hidden one is the archangel Gabriel, who brought Allah's revelations to Muhammad without being heard or seen or recognized.

Just so is the human being, the epitome of creation. The soul, the ruler of the human kingdom, has also two deputies, one invisible and the other material. The hidden one is the will; the material one is the tongue. Human will has the station of Gabriel in human life, bringing revelations from conscience to the pronounced awareness of the tongue. And when the tongue gives expression to what the will has revealed, it is in the position of Allah's messenger, the Prophet.

♦

So seek the meaning of everything within yourself. You will find in your core the truth of his prophecy and the divine message he brought. You will also find, in your very being, the existence of the divine law he established. You will find the similarity in your nature to the things he did and said.

Allah placed at the root of your hand five bones from which five fingers extend, each in five parts.

The foundation of Islamic sacred law is built on five pillars: testifying that there is no god but Allah and that Muhammad is His messenger; daily prayers; paying the poor rate; fasting during the month of Ramadan; and going on pilgrimage to the holy mosque in Mecca.

Like the set of five bones in your hand, there are five daily prayers in Islam, at dawn, noon, afternoon, evening, and night.

The poor rate is due on five properties: cattle, grain, fruits, precious metals, and merchandise.

Islam is established by the grace of the four blessed companions of the prophet, thus a total of five: Muhammad, Abu Bakr, 'Umar, 'Uthman, and 'Ali, Allah's peace and blessings upon them all.

And the members of the blessed household of the Messenger of Allah are also five: Muhammad, peace and blessings be upon him, 'Ali, Fatimah, Hasan, and Husayn, Allah's pleasure be upon them.

Thus Allah has put in your own palm the signs that your salvation depends on living in accordance with the law and in loving and emulating the Prophet and those whom he loved and who loved him.

Islam's five pillars are represented in you by your five senses: your eyes to see it, your ears to hear it, your hands to touch it, your nose to smell its perfume, and your tongue to taste its sweetness. So if you use your five senses the right way, you will come to know that all and everything generates from the five principles of Islam. And by fulfilling those five religious duties you will come to know the truth of everything and receive your share of benefit from everything you see, hear, touch, smell, and taste. Above all, you will be taught the meaning of everything, and you will experience and come to know your Lord and yourself.

Your eyes, in awe of all they see, will invite you in reverence to perform your five daily prayers. The Prophet said:

Prayer is the light of my eyes.

(al-Jami, as-Suyuti)

When you touch something, your hands will know that what they hold is not yours, obeying Allah's orders

Take alms out of their wealth—you will cleanse them and purify them thereby

(Surah Tawbah, 103)

and you will give alms.

When you taste something, your tongue will make you remember those who are hungry and invite you to fast.

When your ears hear someone calling, they will remind you of the call of your Maker, who asked His Prophet to call:

Now give a call to the people to go on pilgrimage.

(Surah Hajj, 27)

And when you smell something, your nose will summon you to seek the breath of mercy of the Most Merciful, as the Prophet once said:

Truly I smell the perfumed breath of the Most Merciful coming from the direction of Yemen. May Allah give you the awareness of what your five senses perceive.

The five fingers of your right hand are given to you to remind you to keep the Blessed Five as guides: Muhammad, the Prophet of Allah, peace and blessings be upon him, and his four companions Abu Bakr, 'Umar,

'Uthman, and 'Ali, and to honor what they hold as truth.

When Allah created our father Adam He placed the light of Muhammad, His first creation, on Adam's forehead. When the angels encountered Adam they paid respect and greeted that light, but Adam was dismayed, being unable to see the divine light of Muhammad shining on his own forehead. So he prayed to his Maker saying:

> O my Lord, I would love to see the soul-light of Muhammad, Your Beloved, whom You will bring to Earth as one of my future sons. So please move it from my forehead to where I might see.

So Allah accepted his prayers, and a spark of the divine light shone from the tip of Adam's index finger. He raised it and said:

> I witness that there is no god but Allah and I witness that Muhammad is His servant and messenger.

That is why the index finger is called "the beautiful one" and is lifted in confirmation of Allah's oneness and uniqueness in Islam.

Then Adam asked his Maker:

> O Lord, will there be any of Your divine light left in me for the birth of other chosen ones?

And the Lord said:

> Yes.

Then Adam saw the light of 'Ali shining from the tip of his

thumb, the light of Abu Bakr on his middle finger, the light of 'Umar on his ring finger, and the light of 'Uthman on his little finger. Thus Allah placed these on the tips of the five fingers of your right hand to remind you of them and to make no distinction between them, nor between them and our Master Muhammad, Allah's peace and blessings upon them, as Allah sets them all together:

> *Muhammad is the Messenger of Allah and*
> *those who are with him...*

(Surah Fath, 29)

so that you hold as true what they held as truth.

Now the five fingers of your other hand are there to remind you of the five members of the Prophet's household: Muhammad, 'Ali, Fatimah, Hasan and Husayn, from whom Allah cleansed all impurity, as He says:

> *Allah only desires to take away all unclean-*
> *ness from you, O people of the household, and*
> *to purify you a thorough purifying.*

(Surah Ahzab, 33)

And the Prophet said:

> This verse is about us, our household—about me, and 'Ali, and Fatimah, and Hasan and Husayn.

(as-Suyuti)

The five toes of each of your feet are also reminders. The five toes of your right foot are meant to keep you mindful of the five-times-daily prayers that Allah has made obligatory for you, for you stand on your feet before your Lord in prayer and in your Lord's service on this earth and in this life. The five toes on your left foot are a reminder to pay your obligatory alms, which are five silver coins for every two hundred you own. As your Maker has put your feet side by side firmly on earth, the importance of prayer and giving to the needy are equal services to your Lord during your life on this earth.

♦

Your Lord also has given to you something in your daily life to remind you of death and resurrection and a taste of the peace or torment you will feel in your grave. That is sleep, and your dreams while asleep.

While asleep, one is as if dead, unable to hear, to see, or to act. Then we dream. In our dream we are given a sight other than what we see awake, and hear with another ear than our usual one. We go and come, eat and drink in another place, another time. You are happy or you suffer, just as if you were waiting in your tomb before the resurrection.

Then you are woken up from your deep sleep, not by your own will nor by your choice, as you will be raised from death on the Day of Judgment whether you like it or not. The ones who deny resurrection, let them sleep without awakening! Let the daydreamers who believe only in this life here on earth deny the trials of the Hereafter. How are they going to answer the Judge on the Day of Reckoning?

Having looked at yourself, now look around you. Do you see that the Creator has created His living creatures of three breeds? He says:

Allah created every living thing from water;
some of them crawl upon their bellies...

such as snakes and worms,

129

*And some of them are those who walk on their
two legs...*

such as men and birds,

And of them are those which walk upon four
(Surah Nur, 45)

as four-legged animals do.

Thus some of them are on their faces as if they are
prostrating in prayer, some of them are erect as in the
standing position in prayer, and others are bent as if bow-
ing down in prayer. Trees and erect stones can only stand.
The creatures that crawl can neither stand nor bow. And
the ones who are on their four feet can neither stand nor
prostrate, yet all of them have no will of their own and
only submit to their Creator's will. And in all they do, they
glorify Him, as well as everything He created.

> *The seven heavens and the earth and those in
> them declare His glory. And there is not a sin-
> gle thing but glorifies Him. But you do not hear
> their glorification.*
> (Surah Bani Isra'il, 44)

The human being is different. To humanity, for whom He
has created the rest of the creation, Allah has given a will.
That is so that you yourself may choose to adore Him in all
the ways the rest of His creation remembers Him:

> *...remember Him standing, bowing, or lying
> down...*
> (Surah al-'Imran, 191)

In you, all the praise of all His creation is manifest. So He ordained for you a way to pray that combines the ways that all things pray, so that you might receive their benefits.

You are at the summit, meant to be the best of all existence. You are the chosen one among all of Allah's servants. You are the purpose of the rest of creation, which He created in your shape and for your sake. And Muhammad, peace and blessings be upon him, is the best among us: Allah's Beloved. That is why He created our father Adam in the shape of the name of Muhammad, and the universe in the form of his blessed being.

♦

Know that all the celestial beings unseen by human eyes are charged to serve the Tree of Being. The purpose of their existence is to toil for its benefit, so that the Tree reaches the heights its Maker destined for it. All this is in honor of its one branch called Muhammad, "the one praised by Allah," and the divine light it contains called Ahmad—the same light Allah first created to separate the light of being from the dark void of nothingness. He placed a spot of light from the sun of Muhammad on our father Adam's forehead. At the sight of it, the angels prostrated:

> *When Allah said to the angels "fall on your faces and honor Adam," they all prostrated but Satan.*
>
> (Surah Baqarah, 34)

And the angels declared:

> Muhammad is the king established on the Throne of Power, forever.

131

They were asked by the Lord to honor the light of Muhammad on Adam's head, and were chosen to be witnesses of what they were shown. They were given the duty to serve the Tree of Being to express their gratitude. So they serve Muhammad, the seed and the soul of the Tree of Being, who bids what his Lord bids, and forbids what his Lord forbids in His kingdom of the universe.

So the angels do what He bids them to do. Some are celestial scribes, writing Allah's words in holy books. Some guard the Tree of Being from impurities. Some are porters carrying the good deeds of Allah's servants. Some transcribe as good deeds the sins of sinners when they repent; others wash clean their faces from the traces of their sins, and some others

> ...ask forgiveness for those on earth.
>
> (Surah Shura, 5)

Yet others are guardian angels who preserve what is written in the destiny of human beings, whether in their favor or against their will. Some distribute people's daily bread so that they will be thankful. Some blow the winds; some drive the clouds; some fill the oceans; some pour the rain, counting each drop; some pull the veil of night over the earth and others shine forth the light of day. Some control people's members from reaching out to sin, some remove calamities in their way. Some help in adorning the gardens of Paradise, and some are charged to feed the fire of Hell.

◆

Thus when everything was set in place and this earth was turned into a living space, the Lord called all

His creatures in and passed the cup of His will around, for all to drink and be pleased.

The first guest who came was Satan, clothed in fancy costumes, displaying his devotion and glorification to His Lord while under this disguise was hidden pride, envy, and lies. He looked around him and saw how beautiful it was, and thought that only he could see and understand. But the beauty he saw only increased his envy, anger, and revolt. All this was still unexposed, hidden under the shiny, fair façade. Just when he had convinced himself of how lowly everything was, made out of earth and water, His Lord ordered him to prostrate in front of Adam, who had been created from wet clay. Now Satan, in revolt, could no longer hide who he really was; he refused Allah's gift offered in the cup of His will, thinking he was too good for it. So he left the good company and the beauty behind and moved into the realms of darkness of imagination, temptation and deceit. In the dark he sought in his memory what he had ever done right, all the knowledge, devotion, and deeds he had boasted about. But he could find nothing. Crushed under the blows of his own doing, losing hope both in the path he took and the ones who followed him, he fell into the chasm of helplessness, without a branch to hold onto in his fall. The single relief he found in his fall was anger and revenge. He screamed in pain:

> *Certainly I will lead them astray and excite in them vain desires and bid them so that they will slit the ears of cattle like the pagans and bid them so that they will alter Allah's creation.*
>
> (Surah Nisa', 119)

133

But the Lord's voice drowned his ugly voice. He said:

> *Truly, over My servants you have no authority.*
> (Surah Hijr, 42)

Perhaps the Devil could have been destroyed there and then—but that was not his destiny. In the darkness of his ignorance, he begged his Lord for a respite, that he might be given the chance to lure the unbelievers into Hellfire. And the Lord granted it to him, that the sinners and the villains might depend on him, and so whenever one of them might slip, he could say:

> *...only the Devil sought to cause him to slip on account of some deeds he did, and certainly Allah pardoned him; surely Allah is forgiving, forbearing.*
> (Surah al-'Imran, 154)

> *...is on account of the Devil's doing...*
> (Surah Qasas, 15)

so that perchance he will repent, saying:

> *My Lord, surely I have done harm to myself, so You protect me...*
> (Surah Qasas, 16)

and perchance his Lord will forgive and

> *...protect him, surely He is the Forgiving, the Merciful.*
> (Surah Qasas, 16)

♦

Time passed, and fate brought Adam and Satan together again at the ford of disobedience. Satan got there because he did not do what he was bidden, and Adam came because he did that which was forbidden. Their destinies brought them together, as was preordained in the divine dispensation. Allah's orders and His will came from different directions. He ordered one thing, yet His will was another. And what He willed blew away that which He commanded.

Yet there were boundaries set for both Adam and Satan. When Satan went beyond bounds, it was ordained that he would stay forever in his transgression. Thus he pitched his tent, tied with ropes of rebellion, in the valley of the fallen from grace, and that became his permanent abode. Meanwhile Adam yearned for the house he had lost in the garden of Paradise. Day and night he mourned, shedding tears, heaping blame on himself.

> *He said: our Lord, we have wronged ourselves;*
> *and if You forgive us not and have no mercy on*
> *us, we shall certainly be of the losers.*
> (Surah A'raf, 23)

And the Merciful heard his plea:
> *Then Adam received words from his Lord and*
> *He turned to him mercifully, for He is oft-*
> *returning to Mercy, the Most Merciful.*
> (Surah Baqarah, 37)

And He forgave our father Adam.

As for the wretched Satan, Allah sent upon him

135

horses of malediction loosed from their reins, sending him the message that he was cast out and sent far from where he was. The Lord said to him:

get down from this place...

(Surah Baqarah, 38)

Adam as well, fallen down from Paradise, in total despair, torn apart in anxiety, begged:

> O my Lord, I tasted the poison of disobedience when I was raised into Paradise, now save me from the fire of desolation in my isolation from You!

And Adam heard the answer to his prayers:

> Fear not till...

> *...the Day of Gathering, wherein is no doubt. A party will be in the Garden and another in the burning fire.*

(Surah Shura, 7)

So when that day came, Adam took the people on the right-hand side and Satan came to take the people on the left-hand side to where they were meant to go.

But at one point Adam and Satan met, there where the paths to the right and the left branched. Since they met, a trace of this companionship remained both in the place they met and in each of them. So the ones whose origin or tendency was to turn left took the path darkened by the black shadow of evil, and to the extent of their blindness in their closeness to Satan they fell into the chasm of disbelief and disobedience, like the one who led them. But those on the right side of Adam were saved.

They saw the truth in the light that shone on Adam's forehead, the light that kept the darkness of evil at a safe distance. Thus what they saw and what they knew saved them from infidelity.

Still in some, the traces of the character of the ones in the darkness, of those on the left side, remained; for before their paths separated they were together for awhile. Yet because their essence was clean at its origin, the dirt stayed on the surface and could not penetrate. Thus those on the right side, too, err and sin, because they were infected by the ones on the left side while they were together for a while. That infection, alas, will never pass.

Yet there is another reason why good people sin. When Allah intended to create our father Adam, He gave orders that a handful of earth be brought from our world; from it, Adam might be created. To do what Allah bid, the Angel of Death came down to earth. But the accursed Devil was already there. Allah had sent him while he was a jinn, before he revolted, together with a group of angels to serve him. For a long time he stayed on earth, performing his devotions. So when the Angel of Death took handfuls of earth for the Lord to make Adam, it so happened that upon some of it Satan had trampled with his feet. When the clay was kneaded together and Adam was made with it, some of his parts were stained with earth soiled by Satan's feet and some other parts were clean. His flesh, his personality, and his desires were afflicted with the dirt under Satan's feet, but his heart was pure, untouched, made of clean earth unsoiled by the wanderings of the Devil. This is the reason that the flesh is the abode of lusts. It bears traces of evil and Satan has power over it because his footprints are on it.

That is also why, when Allah ordered the angels to prostrate in front of Adam, Satan refused, which caused his fall. He thought that a creature made of the mud he had stepped on was inferior to him. And he thought that fire, of which he was made, was far superior to mud. So heed Allah's warning!

O you who believe, follow not in the footsteps of the Devil—and whoever follows in the footsteps of the Devil surely commands indecency and evil. And were it not for Allah's grace upon you and His mercy, not one of you would ever have been pure, but Allah purifies whom He pleases, and Allah is All-Hearing and All-Knowing.

(Surah Nur, 21)

◆

Remember that when the Tree of Being first began to grow, three branches grew from it: one to the right, the branch of the good people on the right-hand side; one to the left, the branch of the unfortunate ones on the left-hand side; and one in the middle, which grew straight up and is the branch of the foremost people, blessed to be the first among Muslims. Allah says:

Those on the right hand, how happy are those on the right hand! And those on the left, how wretched are those on the left! And the foremost are foremost; these are drawn nigh to Allah in the garden of bliss.

(Surah Waqi'ah, 8-12)

The essence in the seed of the Tree of Being is the soul of Muhammad, which spread to all its branches, as the Creator said:

> *We sent you but as a mercy to the whole of creation.*
>
> (Surah Anbiya', 107)

But each branch of the Tree of Being received its share in proportion to its capacity to receive it.

Now the share of the branch of the good people on the right-hand side is the spirit of submission in confirming the example of Allah's Messenger, and in abiding by the law he brought:

> *Those are the ones who follow the messenger-prophet, the unlettered one, whom they find mentioned in both the Torah and the Gospel. He enjoins them good and forbids them evil and makes lawful to them the good things and prohibits for them impure things, and removes from them their burden and the shackles that were on them. So those who believe in him and honor him, and follow the light that has been sent down with him, these are the successful ones.*
>
> (Surah A'raf, 157)

And the portion from the spirit of Muhammad that is the share of the branch growing upwards at the center of the Tree of Being, the branch of the foremost, is to grow toward the Creator, to come close to Him, to be with Him:

*Whoever obeys Allah and His Messenger, they
are with those upon whom Allah has bestowed
favors from among the faithful and the righteous, and a goodly company are they!*

(Surah Nisa', 69)

The branch of the people on the left-hand side also
has a share of Muhammad's spirit. Theirs is protection in
this life on earth from immediate punishment for their
sins:

*And Allah would not chastise them while you
are among them, nor would Allah chastise
them while they seek forgiveness.*

(Surah Anfal, 33)

♦

When the time came for Muhammad, peace and
blessings be upon him, to appear in this world in body and
soul, the shoot of his arrival sprouted up from the seed of
the Tree of Being. Then its roots became firm, its branches grew out, green leaves unfolded. The Lord, without
whose will not a leaf moves, gave the order:

*Be upright as you are commanded, as also
those who walk with you.*

(Surah Hud, 112)

Thus righteousness became the nature and the path of the
Prophet, who was raised by his Lord to a place in Paradise:

*Who, out of His grace, has made him a light in
an abode abiding forever. Therein toil touches
one not, nor does fatigue afflict.*

(Surah Fatir, 35)

As he reached the state of total integrity, he left behind the cares of both this world and the next. In rectitude he was raised from one height to the next, standing upright.

The first place he came to was this material world, where he appeared in flesh and blood. Here he was told:

> *O you who are enwrapped, arise and warn, and your Lord magnify, and your garments purify, and uncleanness shun, and do no favor seeking gain. And for the sake of your Lord, be patient.*
>
> (Surah Muddaththir, 1-7)

And when he did what he was bidden to do and his work was well finished, he heard:

> *This day I have perfected for you your religion and completed My favor upon you and chosen for you Islam as your religion.*
>
> (Surah Ma'idah, 3)

Now

> *Maybe your Lord will raise you to a station of praise.*
>
> (Surah Bani Isra'il, 79)

And he was raised to the level of the Throne of Power, where he will intercede for the sinners on the Day of Judgment. Then he was lifted from the state of temporality to the level of perpetuity, to his place in Paradise

> *...in an abode abiding forever.*
>
> (Surah Fatir, 35)

And finally he was brought to the fourth stage, where he saw his Lord:

141

...One Mighty in Power has shown him the Lord of Strength. So he attained to perfection and he is at the end of the highest level. Then he drew near; drew nearer yet. So he was at the distance of two bows, or closer still. When he revealed to His servant what He revealed, the heart was not untrue in seeing what it saw. Do you then dispute with him as to what he saw? And certainly he saw Him in another descent, at the farthest Lotus Tree, near the Garden of Abode.

(Surah Najm, 5-15)

Only he among all humanity was chosen to be raised so high, to come so near, and to be shown his Lord, so that he could testify to what he had seen with his own eyes. This is because he was the sole purpose for the creation of everything created.

♦

So if we see the whole creation as a Tree, he is the life, the seed of the Tree of Being.

The fruit of a tree is the result of its seed. When the seed is planted, watered, cultivated, it sprouts, grows, a trunk and branches are formed, then the leaves and flowers bud, and it bears fruit. Do you see the seed when you look at that tree? Yet all that grand tree was in that tiny nucleus, from which it came out to be the tree. The seed is also in the fruit, to become trees for all perpetuity.

Likewise the spirit of Muhammad, Allah's peace and blessings be upon him, is hidden in all that is created from the very beginning, and appears in everything when

142

it is born. That is why he said:

> I was a prophet when Adam was still between
> water and earth.

So the destiny of the Tree of Being is in him from the very
beginning, and until the very end.

So speaks the One who created all from nothing,
praising him as the best of creatures. He unfolded the best
when the time came to show it forth. An allegory would be
a merchant of carpets, who puts his best carpet under a
pile, so that the first carpet he laid down will be the last
and best carpet he brings out to show. Thus is the appearance of the master of mankind, our master Muhammad,
Allah's peace and blessings upon him, who was the first
and the best of all creation, but the last to appear and be
born as a man, to lead humanity to salvation.

Now when the One who planted the seed of the
Tree of Being wished to grow in it that branch of prophethood, He fed it with the pure mulch of His compassion,
watered it from the cup of His affection, kept it in the pot
of His protection, and tended it till it grew and flowered.
The perfume of its flowers reached far and wide. The ones
who knew the truth smelled it and breathed in its aroma,
which became nourishment for their souls. This perfume,
when the faithful breathed it, sharpened the light in their
minds. It is transformed into the sweet scent that generates from the lovers of God. Any place one can smell it
becomes a refuge where the rebellious gather; it becomes
a fountain where sinners wash away their filth and
quench their thirst.

Whenever the wind blows from the infernal regions

of the people of the left-hand side—a scorching wind of sin and evil—or whenever there is a tempest of revolt, a flowering branch from that blessed Tree shakes and moves, and covers the evil deeds of the people of the left-hand side. Its green leaves and its fragrant flowers are scorched, and wither. Yet because its root is held firmly in the soil of faith, the Tree of Being is safe. So its branches arch above the ones who sin, keeping them safe from further mischief that might befall them.

Perchance the one burned, fallen, thirsty, hit by the scorching wind of sin, may revive and become aware under the shade of the branch of faith. He will stand up and be upright, cleanse and cool himself with the fragrant dew of mercy dripping from the fading leaves and flowers of the branch that saved him. Then if the regret is sincere, if the intentions are true, if the repentance is accepted, the branch of faith that had wilted will bear new leaves, fresh and green. And a defending spirit will appear and plead for him—the one whom Allah has sent as the intercessor of sinners, about whom Allah Himself takes oath:

> By the star when it sets! Your companion errs
> not, nor does he ever turn away.
>
> (Surah Najm, 1-2)

That branch of mercy, called Muhammad on the Tree of Being, is made out of the material from which all souls are created. But his soul is so pure, so intense, that it illuminates all of our souls. It is described in the secret meaning of the words of the One who created it:

> Allah is the light of the heavens and the earth.
> The parable of His light is as if there were a

*niche and within it a lamp; the lamp enclosed
in glass; the glass as it were a brilliant star; lit
from a blessed tree, an olive, neither of the east
nor of the west, whose oil is well nigh luminous
though fire scarce touch it. Light upon light!
Allah guides whom He will to His light.*

(Surah Nur, 35)

Allah, the Ultimate Light, is a light by Himself, not
a light kindled from other lights. The Prophet of Allah is a
lamp illuminated, lit by His light; a lamp placed in the
niche of the universe, to shed light upon the spirits of all
existing things. The sunlight illuminating physical
appearances depends on eyesight and is not permanent.
When Allah, the source of spiritual light, says:

*O humanity! Verily there has come to you a
convincing proof from your Lord: for We have
sent unto you a light that is manifest,*

(Surah Nisa', 174)

that light is the heart of Muhammad; the glass within
which it shines is his blessed physical being. Thus his
essence shines through his words and actions and presence. His being is pure and transparent, purified with the
fire of the Divine Light in his heart. It shines like a bright
star, to show the way for humankind to follow. The oil of
the blessed olive tree is the spirit of prophethood, an
inexhaustible supply of light that will enlighten souls forever, everywhere. And for every human soul there is a
graded succession of lights of knowledge, wisdom, and
guidance:

light upon light.

The destiny of all people is decided in relation to their closeness to that Light—their following that brilliant star on the path to truth and their living in accordance with the divine law that the Light made manifest.

◆

Allah says that:

> *He sends down water from the skies and the riverbeds flow, each according to its measure; but the torrent bears away the foam that mounts up to the surface. Even so from that ore which they melt in the fire, to make ornaments and utensils therewith, there is a scum likewise; thus does Allah compare truth and falsehood. For the scum disappears, cast out because of its impurity, while that which is for the good of humanity remains on earth; thus does Allah set forth parables.*

(Surah Ra'd, 17)

He likens His Beloved Muhammad to the

> *…water He sent down from the sky according to due measure…*

(Surah Mu'minun, 18)

As water gives life to all things, the light of Muhammad gives life to every heart, and his existence is Allah's mercy upon the universe. So the souls of all persons are enlightened by his light. Their hearts are like the riverbeds where the waters of Allah's blessings from the heavens are channeled and flow. But some hearts are large

146

and some narrow, some are majestic and some are humble. In each riverbed of a heart the waters of life flow—some less, some more, in accordance with what each can hold. These rivers run everywhere and

> *each tribe knows its drinking place.*
>
> (Surah Baqarah, 60)

Then the Lord likens the physical being of Muhammad to the foam that mounts up to the surface when the torrent of pure water flows. That is the symbol of his humanity—eating, drinking, having sex like all other people in their daily lives—all those things that people do day after day, that pass and disappear. Yet what he was sent among human beings to do—to bring them Allah's words, his knowledge, his wisdom, his care, his religion, his intercession—will always remain, in this world and the Next.

Allah in His wisdom created Muhammad as a human being, using both coarse and fine matter to shape his form and character. His appearance was the most beautiful among men, and in character he was the best. He is made as the symbol of a perfect human being so that others may consider him as such and listen to him. His Lord has given him the power to serve, to save, to be with all of humanity and yet to be like them, a man among men, so that he would be able to tell them:

> *I am but a man like yourselves, but it was revealed to me that your God is one God. Whoever expects to meet his Lord let him work righteousness, and in the worship of his Lord admit no one as partner.*
>
> (Surah Kahf, 110)

147

Had he appeared to them in this spiritual aspect, as angel or like a light, no one would have accepted him as Allah's Messenger – nor would the ones destined to fall rejected him. That is why Allah gives him the good news.

There has come to you a messenger from among yourselves. It grieves him that you should perish; ardently anxious is he over you; to the believers is he most kind and merciful.

(Surah Tawbah, 128)

His Lord also gave him power to reach to the celestial realms so that the inhabitants of the unseen heavens might witness his presence. Thus both those spirits who never leave their station near their Lord and the angels who come and go between the heavens and the world recognize him, and his mercy extends to the farthest corners of the heavens as well as to the world.

His Lord raised him above the levels of corporeality and spirituality. Muhammad was brought to a higher level yet. There his Lord placed in him some of His own divinity and lordship in order to increase his affinity to Him through common attributes, so that when He brought him close to Him and spoke to him, he could have the strength to bear it. With that strength he was able to contemplate the Divine Presence, look upon the secrets under the light of his Lord's uniqueness, listen to the signs in His words, breathe in the perfume of His compassion, climb to heights even closer to his Lord's splendor. Thus, leaving the rest of humankind behind, he says:

I am not like one of you. For I have a time with my Lord that none other can enter but my Lord, not even the angels closest to Him or any other prophet whom the Lord sent with a mission.

This is a cup from which none other than he may drink. This is a bride who will unveil to no other. This is a place set only for him at the summit of the four levels to which he was raised. The three levels under him may be attained by others: there those worthy of Allah's generosity may gather wonders.

And what is that Station of Praise to which his Lord promises to raise him when He says:

Maybe your Lord will raise you to a station of praise.

♦

The first step is taken in this world of matter, where he stands among men and inspires people with his serenity; where they profit from the sacred message he brought and are blessed by his mere presence among them, as Allah says about him:

We sent you but as a mercy to the whole of creation.

And he was made to stand at the pulpit and ordered:

O Messenger! Proclaim the message that has been sent to you from your Lord. If you did not, you would not be fulfilling and proclaiming His mission.

(Surah Ma'idah, 67)

He teaches the believers the answers to the questions that will be asked on the Day of Judgment. He advises them how to live their lives in this world, how to cure the ones who are sick at heart, how to give them love.

149

All this and more is performed on the face of this world and in this life at the first step of the Station of Praise given to our Master Muhammad.

◆

The second step to which he is raised is in the Hereafter. When human beings are resurrected and stand at the heavenly trial on the Day of Judgment he will be there to intercede for all mankind.

> *On the Day when the Spirit and the angels stand in ranks, none shall speak except he whom the merciful Lord permits, and he speaks rightly.*
>
> (Surah Naba', 38)

So he stands on his pedestal while the angels silently stand at attention on his right, and all humanity, in great anxiety, in a sea of their sweat, gather around him. And he begs his Lord to forgive them:

O my people! O my people!

he says. And the answer comes:

My mercy, My mercy upon them.

◆

The third step of the Station of Praise leads to Paradise, the eternal home of the righteous. Its inhabitants will receive their due from Muhammad's hands. The celestial maidens will blossom, watching him wander among them. The bejeweled palaces of Paradise will glow when he steps into them. The delights of Paradise will become sweeter, its gardens' flowers bloom, fruits ripen, veils lift, exposing divine secrets. All is bliss and peace, there is no disturbance, all because of his presence.

◆

The fourth step where he alights, the final summit of the Station of Praise, is a place that only Muhammad may reach, Allah's peace and blessings upon him. It is a place where the Beloved Most High is seen. On his ascension:

> *He is at the end of the highest level; then he drew near; drew nearer yet. So he was the measure of two bows or closer still. Then He revealed to His servant what He revealed.*
>
> (Surah Najm, 5)

And Muhammad saw his Lord.

◆

Now the precious fruit of the Tree of Being is ripened. In the oyster of existence, the unique pearl of its secrets is formed.

When Allah pronounced that sacred word *kun!* and the Tree of Being became, the Tree was not the purpose of its own creation. Its purpose was a single fruit. So it was carefully watched and tended and guarded as its flowers blossomed, its fruits formed and ripened, so that one fruit might be carefully plucked to be presented to its Owner.

So it was washed and polished and beautifully decorated like a bride by her sacred attendants, all prepared to be led to its Maker.

151

Then the invitation came. His Lord said:

Rise, O orphan in the house of Abu Talib, the One who wants you with Him has humbled

Himself to receive you.

And His Lord sent the best servant of His celestial kingdom to bring Muhammad to him. And when he came upon him, he found him sleeping in bed. He said:

O Gabriel, where are you taking me?

Gabriel answered:

O Muhammad, the "where" has been removed. There is no more distance or space between you and the One who calls you. I am sent only as a messenger of the Eternal One. I am but one of His servants and we descend to earth

but by the command of your Lord.

(Surah Maryam, 64)

To Him belongs what is before us and what is behind us and what is between these...

Muhammad asked:

What does my Lord want of me?

Gabriel answered:

You yourself are what is wanted by the will of the Creator of all wishes. Everything desired is wished for because there is a trace of you in it,

152

and you are the most desirable because of the one who made you as the best of all creation. You are the clear crystal of the cup of love. You are the pearl of His manifestation. You are the fruit of the Tree of Being. You are the shining sun of knowledge. You are the full moon of God's graces. The earth is spread under your feet only for you to stand on. The beauties of this world exist to celebrate your coming. The cup of love is filled only for you to drink.

So rise up! Feasts are prepared in your honor in the heavens. All its inhabitants have announced your coming among them. The angels are chanting your praises. Although they have seen your name written next to their Lord's in heavenly skies and breathed your spirit, they yearn to see you body and soul.

So come to honor the celestial kingdom as you have honored this lower world. As this barren earth is blessed by the touch of your feet, come stand on the pinnacle of the heavens to bless the angelic realm.

Then Muhammad asked:

O Gabriel, the Generous One who summons me, what will He do with me?

Gabriel answered:

Allah will cover for you your shortcomings in the past and those to come, and complete His favors to you and guide you to success.

(Surah Fath, 2)

Then he asked:

> But are all these favors just for me? What is
> there for my people, my children, my little
> ones? Is not the one who eats alone the worst
> of men?

Gabriel answered:

> *Soon your Lord will surely give to you all that
> will make you well pleased.*

(Surah Duha, 5)

And Muhammad said:

> Well, O Gabriel, now my heart is at ease, I am
> ready to go to my Lord.

Then a strange creature with a human head, a horse's
body, and a peacock's tail came down like lightning and
stood in front of him. Muhammad, peace and blessings be
upon him, asked:

> What is this creature? What am I to do with it?

Gabriel answered:

> It is the celestial steed called *Buraq*, sent to
> carry the lover to his beloved.

And the Prophet said:

> My love and yearning is sufficient to deliver
> me to my Lord; the darkness of night will
> show me the way, and all that I need in my
> voyage is my wish. All praise to Him who will

guide me to Him and let me reach Him! How could a weak creature like this carry the burden of the one who is himself weighed down by the immense love of his Lord and His trust, and by the mountains of revelations of his Lord laden upon?

Allah offered His trust to the heavens and the earth and the mountains but they refused to carry it.

(Surah Ahzab, 72)

As for you, O Gabriel, how can you lead me to Him? You know that beyond the boundaries of the Lotus Tree there are seventy thousand veils of light and fire that will burn you to ashes. Yet there are no boundaries for me, for I have had a moment with my Lord where none other can exist but my Lord and me. As my Beloved bears no resemblance to anything He has created

and none is like Him.

(Surah Shura, 11)

I also am not like one of you. One rides a horse to cover a distance and needs a guide to show the way, but where I am called to there is neither time nor space. The sanctity of my Beloved is here and now, always and everywhere. One need not move, nor be shown where. This said, only the ones who know, know. I am so near to my Lord—

the measure of two bows or closer still...

(Surah Najm, 5)

But come! Let us go.

And the angel Gabriel was in awe. He said:

> O Muhammad, indeed you could have gone alone. I have been sent to you only to serve your splendor and to be a reverent companion. And this beast of burden was brought to you to ride, not so much to transport you, but to honor you and to show your glory. You know that when a sultan invites a guest or a friend, it is customary to send special servants to accompany them and the best beasts of burden for them to ride, in order to show respect and honor them. Thus have we come to fetch you in pomp worthy of your rank.
>
> Certainly whoever believes that the Lord may be reached by covering distances, no matter how unreachably far, is in grave error. And whoever imagines that he is apart from his Lord, even for a moment, has cut himself off from Allah's blessings.

He continued:

> O Muhammad, all the inhabitants of the high heavens are expecting you. The gardens of Paradise have opened their gates, adorned their courts, dressed their hosts; cups are filled with nectar. All is prepared—feasts and festivities for your arrival. This night, through all the

156

creation, belongs to you; all that there is in it is in your favor.

And I have been waiting for this night since I was created. I was created to bring my Lord's messages, and I have been made to reach the ones to whom I bring the message. Yet I have no access to the One who sends the messages. I have neither heard nor seen Him. And I yearn to meet Him! I have tried everything and sought help everywhere. My mind is stupefied, my thoughts are puzzled, my soul is confounded, my heart is burning with longing for Him. It is a secret with no solution. So I tell you about my state hoping that you are my solution, my consolation!

I went and sat in the fields of Infinity, waiting for Him, in vain. I went toward the beginning hoping to find Him: I found that there is no such thing as the beginning. Then I sought Him at the end. I found myself at the same place I had looked for Him at the beginning.

On one of the paths, hoping that it was not another dead end, I came upon Michael: he asked me where I was going. When I told him what I was seeking, he told me my search was in vain. All the gates were closed and all the roads were blocked, for He cannot be reached either in a space where there are distances or in a time where moments are counted, and He is beyond the borders of Infinity. Then I asked what he was doing there and why he had come. He said he was put there in charge of the oceans and rains, to spread them all around where they are meant to go, to measure how much water each is to receive, how much salt there is supposed to be in the seas and how much foam there should be on the top of each wave. Yet he did not know the extent of the Oneness of His Lord. Neither can he count or measure the uniqueness of the One and Only.

Then I wanted to know if Israfil knew, and asked where he was. Michael said that he was at school, studying what is written in the Sacred Secret Tablet—what is to happen and what is to disappear in the whole of creation, as it is

the ordinance of the All-Mighty, the All-Knowing.

(Surah Rum, 39)

Like a child learning to read, he repeats aloud what he reads so that the Teacher can hear. Yet he does not raise his eyes to look at the One who teaches him, out of reverence. His heart as well as his eyes are bent to read universal destiny until the time when he will be asked to rise and blow the Trumpet to mark the end of time.

♦

And Gabriel continued telling his story to Muhammad.

Michael, like him, yearned to see his Lord, but was

158

helpless to find a way. So they decided to go and ask the Throne of Power for guidance—perchance to draw a map to find their way. The Throne, which they thought to be far away, read their thoughts and heard their plea. The whole heaven shook while the Throne trembled with apprehension and said:

> Never speak about such things, don't even think about them! This is such a sacred mystery that it can never be unveiled. Beyond the curtain that hides it there is no door. Your question has no answer: ask whomever you will, no one knows it. Woe to me, that you should come to ask me! Who am I but a creature that became when the two letters K and N drew together when He said *kun*, and everything became? I am here now, but only yesterday I was nothing, without a trace. I am a moment in between. How can I know the end and the beginning? How can one who was no one a moment before, know about the One Eternal, who was before the before and will be after the after?
>
> *He begets not, nor is He begotten; and none is like Him.*
>
> (Surah Ikhlas, 3-4)
>
> With His knowledge of what was before, I was anticipated, then put together by His infinite power. Had it not been for His divine harmony, how could I have been stable enough to be the seat of His power?
> And He mounted up to the heavens when

159

they were only void. And He said to them and the earth:

Come, willingly or unwillingly.

They both said:

We come willingly.

(Surah Fussilat, 11)

For there is only one Law of the One and Only, and all is subject to that Law. Thus

The Merciful is established on the Throne.

(Surah Ta Ha, 5)

He made the Throne and took His seat only to demonstrate His power. I have no knowledge of who sits on me. That I am under Him does not make me any nearer to Him. Even if I am above the heavens I am no nearer to Him than are the lowest depths of His creation. I have been given no power to see what His power contains, nor where it is directed. I am but one of His servants, and all each servant can hope to receive is the service it performs.

Then the Throne of Power continued its own sad story:

I swear by Allah's Power and Glory that I am but a created thing drowned in the oceans of the singularity of the One who created me. I am left in the endless desert of His eternity. Sometimes He rises like the sun in the horizon of His eternity and raises my spirits. Sometimes He draws near me, lowering Himself, to make me accustomed to Him. At another time He covers Himself with the veils of His Might and frightens me in my solitude. Sometimes in my supplication to Him, He whispers to me confidentially and fills me with joy. At yet other times He offers the cups of His love, letting me drink. I get drunk with His love, and when in the sweetness of drunkenness I yearn to see the Beloved, I hear in the language of His singularity:

Never will you see Me.

(Surah A'raf, 143)

and I feel rejected and melt away in awe and yearning for Him. His love tears me apart; I am smitten like Moses. When he wanted to see his Lord, he was told to:

Look at the mountain: if it remains firm in its place, then will you see Me. So when His Lord manifested His Glory to the mountain, He made it crumble, and Moses fell down in a swoon.

(Surah A'raf, 143)

And when he woke up from his swoon he heard a voice saying:

O lost lover, the loveliness you want to see is hidden, veiled from you. No one shall look

161

upon it but the one who is the beloved of the Loved One. He is the chosen one: an orphan whom We brought up.

Glorify Him who carried His servant by night from the Sacred Mosque to the Farthest Mosque, whose precincts We did bless, in order that We might show him some of Our signs.

(Surah Bani Isra'il, 1)

And I am told to go and wait on the way as he ascends toward his Lord. Perchance I will see the only one who is to see his Lord. I hope that his glance may fall on me so that I might be blessed by the one who never gazed at anything without seeing the traces of his Lord.

♦

Then Gabriel said:

O Muhammad, if the Throne of Power is so filled with such ardent desire for you, what else could I be but a servant in your hands?

And he brought him the celestial steed *Buraq* to mount. It took him with the speed of lightning from Mecca to the Jerusalem shrine. There he mounted a second mystical beast called *Mi'raj*, which carried him above the world's atmosphere. Then he rode on the wings of angels from one heaven to another until he reached the seventh heaven. At the seventh heaven Gabriel himself carried the Beloved of Allah on his back up to the Lotus Tree, which

162

bars the way at the border of creation from beyond. That is where Gabriel stopped; he could not go any further. Muhammad, peace and blessings be upon him, said:

> O Gabriel, tonight we are your guest. How could the one who invited us stay behind the one who is invited? Is this a place where a friend abandons his friend?

Gabriel answered:

> You are the guest of the All-Generous Lord. You have been invited here since the beginning of time, while if I move an inch forward from this spot, I will be burned to ashes. Each of us has an appointed station and service beyond which we cannot reach. Allah said:

> *There is none of us but has an assigned place.*
> (Surah Saffat, 164)

Then the Prophet said:

> Then stay where you are. But tell me, do you wish anything of me?
> Yes, he answered.
> When you are taken to your Beloved on that endless path where there are no longer any boundaries, and when you hear Him say, "Here you are, and Here am I!" I beg you to remember me before your Lord.

♦

The archangel Gabriel, peace be upon him, gave a last push to the Beloved of Allah to pierce through the seventy thousand veils of light. Beyond them his fifth transport was waiting for him: a flying carpet made of emerald light, covering all the space between east and west, called *Rafraf*. On this he rode until he reached the Throne. The Throne caught *Rafraf* by the fringes and stopped it and addressed the Prophet, not with words but in the soundless language of love:

> O Muhammad, what exaltation! How long will you sip the pure nectar of this moment reserved just for you? I have known your Beloved to descend to the lowest heavens of the world, yearning for you. This night He has you carried on the wings of His angels and raises you on the flying carpet of His compassion.
>
> *Glory to Him who carried His servant by night.*
>
> (Surah Bani Isra'il, 1)
>
> He will let you see the beauty of His Unity and
>
> *Your heart will not be untrue in seeing what you see;*
>
> (Surah Najm, 11)
>
> the beauty of His perpetuity and
>
> *your eye will not turn aside, nor will it exceed the limit.*
>
> (Surah Najm, 17)
>
> And He will show you the secrets of His celestial kingdom.

He will reveal to His servant what He will reveal.

(Surah Najm, 9)

And will pull you close to Himself, until you are drawn so near,

the measure of two bows, or closer still.

(Surah Najm, 9)

O Muhammad, this is a moment like the moment when someone about to faint from thirst finds a fountain. It is a moment of revival after much pain. I also thirst and pine for Him, but I do not know where to turn to find Him. He created me as the highest and mightiest of all His creation, yet of all His creatures, I am the one who fears Him most. The moment I knew myself, that I am here, I started to shake and shiver in fear and awe of His Majesty. Then He wrote on the legs I stand on

There is no god but ALLAH.

I shook and shuddered even more in awe of seeing His name on me. But when He wrote your name with His, O Muhammad, on His humble Throne – He wrote

Muhammad is the Messenger of ALLAH

I found comfort and security and my agitation stopped.

Just your name written on me brought me all this felicity. Oh! Now what fate awaits me, when I see your beautiful face? O Muhammad, you are sent *as a mercy to the whole creation.*

So do I not have a share of His mercy tonight? I beg you to be a witness on my behalf against those lying men who attribute false worth and eminence to me: save me from Hellfire! I fear some fools have gone astray and imagine that I am a throne larger than the One who has no limits and that He sits on me, while He has no form nor shape; and that I can contain the One who is totally unknown, unknowable, unfindable. Look at me: how could the One whose essence surpasses space and is infinite, whose attributes surpass number and cannot be counted, sit upon me? How could He need me in any way, while He is the One who satisfies all needs and has no need Himself? While He is the All-Merciful whose mercy covers and contains everything, how could I be attached to Him or divided from Him? I am a creature: we are not part of Him, though we are from Him.

O Muhammad! I swear by His Might: although I am placed higher than any other being, I am not any nearer to Him. Nor am I far enough from Him to be separated from Him. I have not the strength to carry Him, neither am I of a size to hold Him, nor can anyone find in me anything that resembles Him. He made me out of compassion, as a favor, as a sign of His benevolence. If He were to make me perish, it would be out of His goodness and justice. I was made by His wisdom and am borne by His Power. How could something that is borne itself carry the One who bears it? So what some say about me is not to be believed. Allah says:

Pursue not that of which you have no knowledge; for everything you see, everything you hear, everything you feel in your heart, will be inquired into on the Day of Reckoning.

(Surah Bani Isra'il, 36)

♦

And the Prophet said to the Throne, in the language of the heart:

O Throne above the heavens, I am much obliged to you, but my obligation to reach my Lord leaves me no time to listen to your laments. Nay! Do not disturb my peace and detachment; do not trouble the purity of my thoughts. This is neither the time nor the place to consider your complaints, nor am I the person to answer them.

Not for the blink of an eye did the Beloved of Allah look at the Throne, nor did he recite to it a single letter of what was revealed to Him.

His eye turned not aside, nor did it exceed the limit.

(Surah Najm, 17)

♦

Then a sixth transport appeared in front of him, a symbol of strength and assurance, a creature called *Ta'yid*: Confirmation. And he heard a voice from above, although he saw no one speaking. The Voice said:

> Your guardian is ahead of you. Here you are:
> you and your Lord!

So he stood amazed, in awe, unable to understand, tongue-tied. Then a drop fell on his lips — sweeter than honey, cooler than snow, softer than cream, more fragrant than musk. And when he tasted it, all the wisdom and knowledge of all the prophets and messengers of Allah was given to him. And his tongue was untied and words of praise and reverence poured from his lips:

> All eternity, and dominion over all and everything, belong to Allah.

He said:

> All grace and praise, all good words and deeds belong to Him.

And he heard:

> *Peace be upon you O Prophet, and the Compassion, Love, and Blessings of ALLAH!*

When all these favors fell upon him, Muhammad remembered all the other prophets and those who love their Lord. He hoped to receive his Lord's blessings for them as well, and begged:

> *May your salutations be upon us and upon the righteous servants of ALLAH.*

and he received them.

(Upon his return, when his ascension to his Lord became known, someone asked his friend Abu Bakr, may Allah be pleased with him, if it was true that he saw his Lord. He said, "Indeed, for I was together with him when he included us, saying 'May Allah's salutations be upon His righteous servants,' and Allah accepted.")

Hearing this exchange of salutations between God and the Prophet, a choir of angels chanted:

> *I witness that there is no god but Allah and Muhammad is His Messenger!*

Over their voices came a call without sound or words. It said:

> *Come closer, O Muhammad!*
>
> (Surah Najm, 8)

Then he drew near, drew nearer yet!

How near did he come to his Lord and how did he approach? He so wished and willed with such burning love that his Lord condescended and descended to him. Or he so annihilated himself for the sake of humankind in intercession accepted by his Lord, that He lifted him up to Himself. Or the devotion of a whole life to the service of the Lord paves the way of Allah's clemency and mercy, leading to Him. Who knows? But certainly the way to one's Lord is not through land and sea and skies, for there is no "where" or "in between" or "time" or "space." Yet

> *He was at a distance of two bows' length or closer still.*
>
> (Surah Najm, 9)

If he had reached only the distance of two bows' length, one could attribute a fixed position to the Lord. But he had to approach "closer still": this negates all place. So he was with his Lord where no place, space, or time existed.

♦

And again a soundless wordless Voice said:
O Muhammad, step in!

And he said:

O my Lord, I see no place to take a step, where should I put my foot?

The Voice answered:

Put your right foot over your left foot, for that is all you are able to see exists. So that all of you know that I am beyond place and time, day and night, distances and limits, earth and skies, all that you know and will ever know.

Then the Voice said:

O Muhammad, look!

He looked, and saw an immense light everywhere and under his feet. He asked:

What is this light?

The Voice responded:

This is not a light. It is the Gardens at the summit of Paradise. As you were raised toward Me, it rose to have your feet rest upon it, for being under your feet is the redemption of Paradise, its deliverance from the misconception of those who think that it is not here, now. Now you know it has always existed, it is here now, and will be here when all else will disappear.

O Muhammad, while you were enclosed within time and space, while there was a "here" and a "there," I sent you Gabriel to be your guide and *Buraq* to ride. But when place and time are left behind and you are hidden from the eyes of *jinn* and men, when there is no "here" or "there" or "in between" and the two arches of the two bows facing each other meet and became a circle, there is no longer a distance of two bows between you and Me... I, who am now your Guide.

O Muhammad, I open the gate for you and I lift the veils and speak to you as I have never spoken to anyone. This gift I bestow upon you, because you wholly believed in Me and declared My Unity taking Truth on faith, without knowing Me. So now, bear witness after having come and met Me.

Having heard this the Prophet said:

I take refuge in Your Indulgence from Your Penance.

And the Voice said:

That is not a proper thing to say for the one who confirms Our Unity, although it may be a proper supplication for the sinners of your community.

And Muhammad said:

How can I praise You as You are, as only You can praise Yourself?

The Voice said:

If your tongue cannot express what you will, then We will give you a

tongue of Truth

(Surah Maryam, 50)

and it will not

speak out of desire.

(Surah Najm, 3)

And if your eyes cannot fix on the real reality, I will always guide them, so that your eyes turn not aside, nor exceed the limit of Truth.

And I will surround you with a glow, and in that light you will see My beauty everywhere. And you will have such quietude that you may always hear what I say. And I will teach you the language of the soul, which will make you comprehend the mystery of your being lifted to Me, and the wisdom of Our meeting.

And in that language of the soul, which He taught him, Allah said:

O Muhammad!

I have sent you as a witness and a bearer of good tidings and as a warner.

(Surah Ahzab, 45)

A witness must witness that to which he bears witness. It is not permissible for him to bear witness to something he has not seen. That is why I have shown you My Paradise, which I prepared for My friends, and My Hell, which I prepared for My enemies.

I will make you contemplate My might and gaze upon My Beauty, so that you may know that in My perfection I am free and exempt from anything that may be conceived as similar or resembling, limited or measurable, that has a shape or size or may be counted in numbers, or may be reached for or joined with, come to or left behind, seen or touched or any other thing imaginable.

O Muhammad! I created the creation so that they might know Me. But men are misled about Me. Some claim:

Ezra is the son of Allah

(Surah Tawbah, 30)

and that

the Hand of Allah is tied up.

(Surah Ma'idah, 64)

Some claim that I have a wife and

The Messiah is the son of Allah.

(Surah Tawbah, 30)

173

Some attribute partners to Me and worship as
His partners other than Allah...

(Surah Yunus, 66)

Some give Me a bodily form and imagine
Me doing things as they do. Some think of Me
as a physical thing, some think of Me as light,
and others disagree with those who make
images of Me and decide that I am nothing,
nonexistent. Now know who I am. I have
opened My gates and lifted My veils: look
upon Me, O My beloved! Do you see anything
reminiscent of what they claim?

What he saw was a light: everywhere, not coming
from anywhere, a light that lights itself, singular,
nothing else visible in it, impenetrable, unreachable,
unchangeable, neither on anything nor in anything, nor
anything in it; without shape, without form, without
space, not made out of anything, unlike anything: a light
with which everything is to be seen.

Nothing is like Him, and He is All-Hearing,
All-Seeing.

(Surah Shura, 11)

And when he was eye to eye, face to face with his Lord,
and his lips were one with His Lips, his Lord told him:

O My beloved, there are secrets you may know
that none other should; they should not be
told. This moment cannot ever be shared. No
one else ever came here or ever will

174

and then

He revealed to His servant what He revealed

(Surah Najm, 10)

which will stay a secret between Him, and him.

O Allah, bestow Your peace and blessings and Your grace upon the noblest of Your creation, our guide and master Muhammad—the ocean of Your divine light, the source of Your secrets, the voice that vouches for Your Oneness; the purpose of the creation, the adornment of Your kingdom, the treasure house of Your compassion, the straight path of Your ordinances; the sun of the days of Your Paradise, the eye with which Truth is seen, the joy of the ones who love You, the mirror from which Your light reflects.

O Lord, bless him with the power of being one with You forever, so that the knots in our hearts are undone, so that we are freed from all afflictions, so that our hopes are fulfilled, so that we reach our goal. And may Your graces and blessings upon him be everlasting, as a reflection of Your eternity. And may You be pleased with him, as he is pleased with You, and may humble humanity share in Your pleasure, and May You be pleased with us.

Allah is sufficient for us, and He is the best defender.

(Surah al-'Imran, 173)

There is no force nor power but through Allah, the Greatest on earth below and in the heavens above, the Highest One above the whole of the created universe.

O Allah! Bestow your peace and blessings upon our master Muhammad and upon his family and companions. *Âmin.*

And here our words on the Tree of Being are done.☙

APPENDIX

by Shaykh Tosun Bayrak

Ibn 'Arabi's work, *The Tree of Being*, is an inspired declaration of his deep love for the Prophet.

We must realize that love is not within human will, nor can a person be forced to love. But if we wish to love someone, it helps to know the one whom we wish to love.

May Allah inspire our hearts with the love of our Master Muhammad, peace and blessings be upon him, above anything else we love, for he said:

> As long as you do not love me more than anything else, your faith is not complete.

To help the reader to know him, we have attempted to offer a description of him: a drop from the ocean!

ON THE HOLY
PROPHET MUHAMMAD
peace and blessings be upon him

MUHAMMAD, PEACE BE UPON HIM, is the last and the seal of all the prophets. All the others were sent to particular people at a certain time, but the Beloved of Allah, the best of all creation, was sent as God's mercy upon the universe, as the prophet of all humanity until the end of time, and afterwards in the Hereafter. His prophethood preceded the creation of Adam, the first man and the first prophet, for he himself said:

> I was a prophet when Adam was between water and clay. (Bukhari)

God created the Light of Muhammad, his soul, as His first creation. He created all and everything from the Light of Muhammad. Thus the essence of all prophethood was always present in his first-created soul, but he declared his prophethood in the body at the age of forty. It is wrong to think that he became a prophet at the age of forty.

His Miracles

Since miracles are not ordinary but supernatural, God has given them to prophets to convince ordinary people of their superiority. For Prophet Salih, God made a camel from a block of stone. For Prophet Abraham, He made the fire into which Nimrod threw him turn into a fragrant rose garden. He made the staff of Prophet Moses turn into a dragon as he cast it to the ground, and made sweet water pour from twelve corners of a rock to quench the thirst of his people. God made iron soft for Prophet David, and from it he molded armor to wear against his enemies; He placed mountains and birds under his orders, and they sang the praises of God with him. He made the *jinn*, birds, beasts, and winds obedient to Prophet Solomon, and taught him their language, so that he could command the wind to carry him a month's distance in a day. His Lord caused Jesus to give life to a bird made out of clay, to make the blind see, to cure leprosy, and to revive the dead.

Just as John the Baptist and Christ had done before him, the Prophet Muhammad spoke as soon as he was born. He made prostration, and people heard him begging his Lord: "O my people, O my people, Lord save my people!" and then he said: "I bear witness there is no god but God and that I am the Messenger of God." By the permission of God he split the full moon in half to convince the faithless in Mecca—but in vain. Trees and rocks spoke and saluted him, and bore witness to his prophethood. When on many occasions there was no water to drink and wash, water poured from between his blessed fingers, enough to quench the thirst of hundreds of his people.

But the greatest of all miracles was the Prophet Muhammad's Night Journey to meet his Lord. He went in an awakened state, in the company of the archangel Gabriel, from the Holy Mosque in Mecca to the Aqsa Mosque in Jerusalem. There he led the souls of all the prophets in prayer before traversing the seven heavens and passing the Lotus Tree that marks the furthest limit of creation. Passing beyond, he met his Lord in a realm that no other human being or angel has ever entered. He spoke ninety thousand words with God. Then he returned to this world. The bed he had left was still warm, and a leaf he had brushed on arising was still moving.

No one before ever saw God in life, nor will anyone else but our Prophet ever see Him. Although it is promised to the faithful in Paradise to see God as clearly as the full moon, only God knows if it is with the eyes in the head that we shall see, or with the eyes of the heart.

Yet a greater miracle even than this was the Holy Qur'an, the word of God, which came from the blessed lips of the Holy Prophet. No one before its revelation, and no one until the end of time, could write a single verse equaling its meaning and beauty. Its meaning is so deep and vast that if all the oceans were ink and all the heavens were paper, and all of them were employed in writing out its mysteries, they would be exhausted before the meaning of the Qur'an was exhausted. All knowledge of the visible and invisible realms, of the world and Hereafter, of things past and things to come, all the cures for all human ills are in it. And it is constant: not a word or a letter has changed since its revelation, nor will it change until the end of time.

It is an obligation upon everyone to accept the prophethood of Muhammad, God's peace and blessings be upon him, and also to know about his life.

His Birth

Muhammad, peace and blessings be upon him, was a human being who came into this world through a father, 'Abdullah, and a mother, Aminah. He was born in the city of Mecca in Arabia, during the earlier hours of the forenoon on a Monday, the twelveth of Rabi' ul-Awwal in the Year of the Elephant (570AD), fifty-two days after the armies of Abrahah, who had intended to destroy the Ka'bah with his elephants, were defeated.

He was from the family of Bani Hashim of the tribe of Quraysh, and a descendant of Prophet Ishmael, the son of Prophet Abraham, through the tribe of Bani Kinanah. He grew up as an orphan. His father died before he was born and his mother died when he was a young child. Thus instead of calling on his parents when he was in need, he called upon his Lord.

He was unlettered. He never had a man as a teacher, yet he was the wisest of men, for he had the Lord as his teacher.

His Spiritual Status

Allah Most High, in His mercy, sent His Beloved as a mercy upon the universe. Muhammad, peace and blessings be upon him, was the one whose soul was Allah's first creation, created from the Light of Allah, as he himself confirmed, saying to us:

> The first creation that Allah created was the light of your prophet from His Light.
>
> (Bayhaqi)

> And he was the first of all prophets as he said:
> I was a prophet when Adam was between water and clay.
>
> (Bukhari)

182

He was also the last of all prophets, as he said:

> I was the first of prophets in creation, and the
> last of them in Resurrection.

Such is the one about whom Allah says,

> *Certainly a messenger has come to you from*
> *among yourselves, grievous to him is your*
> *falling into distress, most solicitous for you,*
> *merciful to the believers...*
>
> (Surah Tawbah, 128)

May Allah inspire our hearts with the love of our Master
above anything else we love, for he said:

> As long as you do not love me more than any-
> thing else, your faith is not complete.
>
> (Bukhari)

We must realize that to love is not within our will, nor can
we be forced to love. But one can wish to love someone,
and it helps to know the person whom one wishes to love.

His Nature

His physical appearance. He was neither tall and lanky
nor short and stocky. He was slightly taller than medium
height. He had broad shoulders and a broad high chest.
He was strongly built; his chest and stomach were flat and
firm. No part of his flesh was loose. On his back, between
his shoulders, was the Seal of Prophethood. His bones
were heavy and his wrists were long. His thighs were lean.
His complexion was white tinged with reddishness, like a
flower. His skin was soft. When he took his shirt off of his
shoulders, the color of his body was like cast silver. Fine

hair covered the line from mid-chest to navel. He had no hair on his chest, but his arms and shoulders were hairy.

He had a large head and a round face. He had large black eyes, the lids of which seemed to be outlined, and he had long lashes. The whites of his eyes were slightly pink. He had wonderful eyesight. He could see in the dark as well as he could see in daytime.

He had a high forehead and thick eyebrows separated in the center, where there was a visible vein. It used to swell when he got angry, and his temples would turn red.

His hair was jet black, with about twenty white hairs. It was neither curly nor straight, but moderately wavy. He braided his hair. When he let it loose, its length would not pass his earlobes. He would part it in the middle.

He had long sideburns and a thick beard and moustache, which he shaped by clipping and thinning it, keeping his moustache above his lips. He would wash his beard often, and perfume it with musk. He used often to gently hold his beard when he was sad and pensive.

His face was not plump, his cheeks were not round. He had a straight nose and a rather large mouth. His neck was like a column of silver. His teeth were perfectly white and even, with a slight space between them. When he smiled delicately, they shone like pearls, and one could see his eyeteeth. When he laughed he used to put his hand in front of his mouth.

When he was happy, his face shone like the moon, and when he spoke, it seemed as if a light emanated from between his teeth. He had big but beautiful hands and feet. The palms of his hands and the soles of his feet were firmly padded. He had no hair on his feet. When he washed them, the water didn't stay on them.

He walked with a firm gait, slightly leaning forward as if he were holding a staff, and without any evident effort, as if striding downhill. He walked very fast. People would run behind him, and could not keep pace with him. When people who were weak were his companions, he slowed down or made them ride animals of burden and let them follow behind, and he prayed for them.

He did not look to the side, and never turned to look behind him. Even when his robe would get caught in a bush he would not turn and look. Others who saw it would come and free it. He insisted that his companions walk in front of him rather than behind him. His face was the most beautiful of human faces. His form was the most beautiful to be found among men; so was his character.

His manner. He was the most generous, the most valorous, the gentlest. He cast his eyes down more often than up, and appeared shyer than a well-sheltered young girl. When someone came to him with a happy face, he would take his hand.

When gifts were brought to him, he would ask if they were alms or gifts. He would accept the gifts and decline the alms. Yet the gifts did not stay in his hand or his house for very long. He would give them away.

He used to take off his shoes when he sat down, and bend and gather the skirt of his robe. He would always sit on the floor with his knees pulled up to his chest.

He would stay silent for long periods and laugh little, yet he had a sense of humor and liked to see others smile. When he met with his people he would first give them the greeting of peace and blessings and then embrace them. Caressing them, he would pray for them.

When he was with other people he would not leave their company until they left, and when he took someone's hand, he wouldn't withdraw his hand until the other person released it. When someone whispered into his ear something that he did not want others to hear, he would not pull his face away until the other did.

He was very compassionate and loving, especially to women and children. When he promised something to someone, he would fulfill his promise without fail at the first opportunity.

When he sat with his people, they sat around him in a circle, and in love and fascination they would be so quiet and still that if a bird had sat on their heads, it would not have flown away.

As he spoke, he often lifted his eyes to the heavens. When something that greatly pleased him was announced to him, he would immediately prostrate as a gesture of thankfulness to Allah, and his face would shine like the full moon. When he began speaking he would always smile.

In all his relationships he never caused two people to be angry at each other or to have to defend themselves. Whenever he was asked for something, he would give it if he had it. If he did not have it, he would not refuse, but would not respond. He never said no. When he was asked to do something, if it was possible he would say yes. If it was not possible, he would keep silent. He did not approach nor listen to people from whom he expected to hear bad talk, and he did not accept people's talking against each other.

He spoke very clearly, separating each word, so that one could easily count each word if one cared to.

When he spoke publicly he would repeat each sentence three times to make sure that it was well understood, but he would not repeat it again.

He did not like people who were loud and rude. He preferred people who spoke softly. He also did not like people who asked too many questions.

He smelled beautiful. From his perfume, which would precede him, people knew that he was coming. Since his perfume lingered, people would know when he had been in a place.

His displeasure. When he knew of something bad someone had done, he wouldn't give the person away by mentioning his name, saying "Why is so-and-so doing this?" Instead he would say, "Why do people do this?"

When he was not pleased it became evident on his face. He would lift his face to the heavens and pray *sub-hân Allâh il-'Azîm. Yâ Hâyyu yâ Qayyûmu bi-rahmatika astaghîthu,* (God the Majestic is exalted beyond this. O Living and Ever-Transcendent One, by Your mercy: I seek help.)

He was terrifying to the enemies of Islam.

What he hated most was lying. Even in his own household, if someone told the slightest untruth, he would not speak with that person until he or she repented.

When he was angered his temples would become flushed and the vein between his eyebrows would swell, and he would sweat. To appease his wrath he would sit if he had been standing, lie down if he had been sitting, get up and make two cycles of prayer, and his anger would pass.

When, rarely, he was really wrathful, no one would

187

dare to come close to him except his son-in-law, Hadrat 'Ali (may Allah dignify his countenance). Yet to the worst of his people he appeared loving and gentle in his words and his being, and so gained their hearts.

When he did not see one of his people for three days, he would ask after that person, and if absent people could not come, he would go to them. When he did not know the name of one of his people he would address him as "O son of Allah's servant." When he would take someone's hand to say farewell, he would not withdraw his hand before the other withdrew his, and he would pray, "I entrust you to Allah's care, you and your faith and your trust and your deeds and your end." When he was about to leave a gathering, he would say *astaghfirullâh* (I seek God's forgiveness) aloud twenty times, and lift himself up, supporting himself with one arm.

His dressing. Whatever he did, he did well.

He liked to wear a simple robe, the skirt of which was down to his heels, and the sleeves down to his fingers. He would gather his robe so that it hung in front, but lifted it behind when he walked so that it would not drag.

He washed and mended his own clothes.

He would cover his head and most of his face. He would wear a white cap, and sometimes wrap a turban around it so that the end of the turban would hang down his neck between his shoulders.

He was very careful of the cloth that was used in his robes. If it contained silk, he would discard it. He liked wool. He had a woolen robe that he wore on Fridays and holy days. The robe he liked most was made from colored Yemeni cloth. The colors he liked best were green and yellow.

188

When he had a new dress made, he would give it a name and wear it on Fridays. When he wore anything new, he would praise Allah and make two cycles of prayer in thankfulness, and immediately give his old dress to a poor person.

When groups of foreigners came to visit him, he would wear his best clothes, and ask his companions to do the same.

He wore treated leather sandals with a thong between the toes, which he liked to be the size of his feet, not larger. He wore silver rings on both his right and left hand, and interchanged them. Sometimes they would have a carnelian set in them.

When he dressed and washed and combed himself, in fact in all his doings, he liked to start from the right. When he put on his sandals and robe he would dress his right foot and right arm first. In taking them off, he would remove the left foot and left arm first.

He disliked bad smells.

He bathed on Fridays with five buckets of water. Sometimes he and one of his wives would share the same tub and the same water. He used depilatory every month on the genital area, each time washing it thrice, and then would depilate his armpits. He would cut his fingernails every two weeks. He fumigated himself with incense. He liked to use the *miswak*, a stick of wood beaten into fibers at one end, as a toothbrush. He carried it with him, and used it to clean his teeth very often. He wouldn't enter the houses of his wives, nor go to bed, without brushing his teeth.

He used to sweat a lot, but his sweat smelled of roses. He would perfume and oil his hair and beard with musk. When someone offered him perfume he would never refuse, and would apply it. Sometimes he would go into his wives' rooms and look for perfume.

When he used perfume he poured it into his left hand and first applied it to his brow, then around his eyes, then to his head. He liked best the smell of the balsam flower.

His eating and drinking. He liked to drink cool and sweet drinks, and among these he liked best water sweetened with honey. He also liked milk. When he drank he would breathe before swallowing, and say *bismi Llâh ir-Rahmân ir-Rahîm* (In the Name of Allah, the Beneficent, the Compassionate). After each swallow he would say *al-hamdu li-Llâh* (Praise is due to Allah). He would take only two or three swallows in this way.

He had a glass cup from which he drank. He liked to drink water from its source. Sometimes he would send people to particular springs, wells, and fountains where there was good water, and he would pray for the people who brought the water to him. He would drink *Zamzam* water each time he went to Mecca; he would carry it himself or ask his people to bring it to him.

He liked to sit and watch running water and greenery.

He kept his water in covered containers.

He ate little, and if he ate in the evening he wouldn't eat in the morning. He ate only when he was hungry, and stopped eating before he was full.

He fasted often. In addition to the month of Ramadan, the month in which he fasted the most was Sha'ban. The ninth of Dhul-Hijjah, the day of 'Ashurah, the first three days and the first Monday of each month he passed fasting. It was rare if he did not fast on Fridays.

Sometimes to appease his hunger pangs he would tie a flat stone against his stomach. Sometimes he would fast for days without breaking the fast, but he would forbid others to do that.

He never kept anything for tomorrow. Sometimes neither he nor his family had anything to eat for days. They often ate barley bread.

When he broke his fast at sunset, he would first eat a date or two or drink water before he made his sunset prayer.

When he ate, he sat on the floor and set his food on the floor; he never leaned on anything while he ate. He washed his hands well before and after eating. He started the meal by saying *bismiLlâhi* (in the name of God). He ate with the three fingers of his right hand. He ate what was on his side of the plate; he never reached for a morsel in the middle of the plate, and did not approve when other people who ate with him from the same plate did it. He did not start eating a warm dish until it cooled. In fact, he did not like warm dishes. He said, "Eat cold food, because it has the blessing of abundance. If you are heedful you will see how much more you must eat when you eat warm food…"

He never blew on his food to cool it, nor did he blow into his cup when he drank. He liked to break his fast with fresh dates or something fire had not touched.

He liked dates: he liked to hold them in his hands attached to their branches in bunches and eat them one by one. He ate them with bread, with watermelon, with cucumber, with cream, and he would say, "What a blessed fruit!" Even when there was a worm in a date, he wouldn't throw it away; he would clean the worm out and eat the date. He started his meals with dates and finished them with dates.

He liked sweet things. He liked honey, and *halwa* (a sweet made with cereals, sesame oil, and syrup), and raisins.

He ate meat. The meat he preferred was the front part of the sheep, especially the shanks of the front legs. He disliked eating the internal organs of the animal. He refused to eat the kidneys, although he did not forbid others to eat them.

Among vegetables he liked squash and cucumbers. He disliked onions, garlic, leeks and such things as leave a smell on the breath, for he spoke with angels, and did not like to offend other people in congregations.

He accepted all invitations to dinner, even from a slave, where he may have eaten stale animal fat with old barley bread. He ate everything that was offered to him if he was hungry. He started eating only after others started. After each meal he said *al-hamdu li-Llâh* (praise is due to Allah), and prayed for his host and the ones who had shared the meal.

His sleeping. He went to bed after the night prayer, awoke in the middle of the night to pray, and slept again until before the morning prayer. He liked to take an afternoon nap. His eyes slept but his heart did not sleep.

His bed was a piece of felt. Sometimes he used a straw mat thrown on the hard floor, which marked his blessed side when he lay upon it. The mat was not bigger than the size of a grave.

Before he went to bed, he would always recite

192

Surah Kafirun and one or more of the following: *Surah Mulk*, *Surah Sajdah*, *Surah Bani Isra'il*, and *Surah Zumar*. He would not go to bed without taking an ablution and cleaning his teeth. He kept his *miswak* (toothbrush stick) next to his bed and would use it when he woke up.

He slept with his head turned in the direction of the Ka'bah. He slept on his right side and used his right hand as a pillow, placing his palm under his cheek. Before he fell asleep, he would pray:

> O my Sustainer, I live with Your name; I die with Your name. (Bukhari)

He then he would repeat three times:

> On the day of Resurrection, save me from Your wrath. (Bukhari)

He breathed heavily when he slept.

His family relations. He loved and cherished his wives. Whether they were young or old, beautiful or less beautiful, he treated them equally. When he got married or performed a wedding ceremony, he distributed dates to the wedding guests. He liked to give gifts, and advised his people to do the same. He would say that giving gifts brought people together.

He smiled when he spoke, and showed care and compassion to the members of his household. He did not touch even the hand of a woman from outside his family. He would talk to, amuse, and play with his wives. He would show them affection, kiss and caress them even when he was fasting. He did not consider his ablution lost as a result, and would make his prayers without renewing his ablution.

He divided his time equally among his wives. He was able to visit all of them in a day or a night and satisfy them all. He would send word to the wife whom he intended to visit.

He had a yellow bed sheet, dyed with saffron, which was always kept proper and clean. He took this with him to sleep on with his wives. The wife with whom he spent the night would wash and fold it for him. He would take ablution and say *bismi Llâh* (in the name of God), when he came close to his wives; he asked them to recite *subhân Allâh* (God is exalted above everything), *al-hamdu li-Llâh* (praise is due to God), and *Allâhu akbar* (God is greater) thirty-three times each. When they made love, they were careful to keep their sexual parts chastely covered. During intercourse he usually stood on his knees. They took a total ablution immediately afterwards; rarely, in dire conditions of cold and fatigue, he delayed ablution and slept until before prayer time. He would not sleep with his wives when they had their periods, but he would still show them physical affection.

He helped with the household chores. He cleaned, washed, mended, and milked the sheep. No work was beneath his dignity. He took his wives out, and brought them and his children to special holiday prayers. When he traveled or left for battle, he would not choose one of his wives to accompany him; rather he would let those who wished to go draw lots to decide who would accompany him.

When his wives became ill, he took care of them and cooked soup for them saying, "Drink! This will cleanse the pain and sadness in the heart of the sick as water cleanses the dirt of a person's body."

He would pray for them when they were ill, reciting *Surah Falaq* and *Surah Nas* three times. When one of his wives was sick with an infectious disease, especially of the eye, he would not go close to her, fearing to infect others.

When his wives wanted something, he never said no, but brought them what they wanted as soon as he could. If he was worried about forgetting it, he would tie a string to his little finger or to his ring. He would pray for his wives and sacrifice sheep for them. When they were annoyed, he would be gentle with them. Once when Hadrat 'A'ishah (may Allah be pleased with her) was annoyed, he gently caressed the tip of her nose and called her "my little 'A'ishah," and asked her to pray so that her anger would subside.

He was wonderful with children. He saluted them like grown-ups, talked to them, caressed their heads, and hugged them. He would stand up, the gesture of respect, when his daughter Hadrat Fatimah (may Allah be pleased with her) came to see him, and he would kiss the top of her head. He always wanted children around him during prayer time in the mosque. His grandchildren would climb on his back while he prayed and he did not mind. He loved all of his people, but he loved the very young and the very old most of all.

His possessions. He possessed little, did not keep things long, and gave them away. He liked to give names to his belongings. He had a mirror he called *Mudillah* (Misleader), and a pair of scissors he called *Jami'* (Uniter). He had a water pitcher called *Mamshuq* (Thin and Tall) and a sleeping mat called *Quzz* (Shunner of Impurity). He had a glass cup and two *kohl* containers. He used to put *kohl* on his eyelids every evening three times from each container. He had a wooden perfume bottle. He always had one new robe, which he wore on Fridays. He had one towel. He had a heavy iron basin that it took four people to lift, called *'Unarah* (Well built), and an iron cooking pot with four rings as handles.

He kept a maid named Hadirah. When he addressed her, he would ask her "What would you like?" He never complained about the service of the ones who served him.

He had a donkey named *Ya'fur* (Gazelle) that he often rode without a saddle. He had two horses, a roan named *Murtajaz* (Spontaneous) and a black named *Sakb* (Swift). He had a mule, *Duldul* (Vacillating) and a she-camel, *Kaswah* (Split ears). He loved and cared for his animals. When he left this world, *Kaswah* ran away into the desert. Every night she would come to the mosque looking for him, crying and hitting her head on the stone steps. One night she killed herself by hitting her head on the stone walls of the mosque.

He had a sword called *Dhul-Fiqar* (Double-pointed) with a decorated silver handle with a silver ring. He had a bow called *Dhus-Sadad* (Mark-hitter) and a quiver for his arrows called *Dhut-Tamam* (Always full) He had a short spear called *Nab'ah* (Arrowwood) and a shield called *Zaqan* (the Beard).

His devotions. He had two *muezzins* who called the prayer five times a day, Hadrat Bilal and Ibn Maktum, who was blind.

What he liked best in this world was *salât*, the ritual prayer. He made his prayers seeing his Lord. That is

196

why he asked his people to do their prayers as they saw him do them, not as he did them. It would have been impossible for anyone to pray as he did. The people whom he liked most were the people who were constant in their devotion. When he led the prayer, he made it short and easy. When he prayed alone, he made it long. He would stand at prayer all night until his blessed feet were swollen.

When the weather was cold, he prayed early. In the heat of the summer, he delayed his prayers. When he sent someone to a place as governor or *imam*, he would warn them:

> Speak not long. Long talk has the effect of a sorcerer's spell. Make your preaching short and make things easy for people, not difficult. Give them good tidings, not threats of punishment.
>
> (Bukhari)

He performed his ablution before every prayer. When he made ablution he would try to conserve water. He would put aside a little and sprinkle it on the place where he would put his head in prostration. When he washed his hands, he would move his rings so that water got under them. When he washed his lower arms up to the elbows, he rubbed well up above them. He would wash and rub his earlobes and then take a handful of water, put it under his chin, rub his beard well and comb it with his fingers. When he washed his feet, he rubbed between his toes with his little finger. He liked to dry his hands and arms after ablution by air and rubbing, rather than by drying them with a towel. After the ablution was complet-

197

ed he used to make two cycles of private prayer before he did his prayers in congregation. He did not permit anyone to assist him when he performed his ablution. He would not let them pour water or even hand him a towel. Neither did he like to ask people to serve him.

When he prayed, his color would change: sometimes he would grow pale, sometimes he would flush. At the time of the morning prayer, the maids of the people of Medina would come to the mosque with water pitchers: he would dip his fingers in the pitchers and bless them. After finishing the morning prayer, he would sit and offer private prayers with his face turned toward the Ka'bah until sunrise. Then he would turn to the congregation and say:

> If anyone is sick, let me go and visit him. If anyone is dead, let me assist at his funeral. If anyone has dreamed, let him come and tell me his dream.

When he stood up to pray, he would raise his hands, open his fingers with palms facing forward and say *Allâhu akbar* (God is greater). Then he would lower his hands and hold his left hand with his right hand. When he bent from the waist in prayer, he would place his hands with open fingers right above his knees; his back would be so straight that if you poured water on it, it would remain there and not run off.

Nothing prevented him from praying, nor from doing so at the proper time. When he traveled, however, he would make the *salât* of noon and afternoon together at the time of afternoon prayer, and he made the evening and night *salât* together at the time of night prayer. In fact he was in constant prayer, for he never forgot Allah, but remembered Him at each breath.

He liked to pray in gardens and open spaces. He usually prayed on a treated sheepskin or a straw mat. He usually took off his shoes when he prayed, but sometimes he kept them on. He would make extra prayers between the afternoon and evening times, but forbade others to do so. He would do two cycles of private prayer before the noon congregational prayer and two cycles afterwards, two cycles before afternoon prayer, two cycles after evening prayer, and two cycles after night prayer.

Sometimes during the prayer it would appear that he was looking around him out of the corners of his eyes. Indeed he sometimes saw what was happening behind him as if it were in front of him. When he led prayers, men stood in rows behind him; behind them stood the children, and behind the children stood the women.

Sometimes he remained so long in prostration that he momentarily fell asleep from fatigue. He would get up and continue his prayers. Although sleep breaks an ablution, his eyes slept, but his heart did not sleep.

He kept the fingers of his hands spread apart when he raised them at the beginning of the *salât*, and when he placed them on his knees, when he bent from the waist, and when he sat on his knees, but he held them tightly together when he pressed them on the floor next to his face during prostration. He raised his elbows so high so that one could see the white of his armpits.

At the end of the formal prayers, during his private supplications, he prayed first for himself, and then for those who were in urgent need. When he prayed for someone, his prayer affected not only that person, but his family, children, and grandchildren as well. When he made his supplications, he opened his hands with palms facing his face; sometimes he raised them high toward the heavens. When he finished supplicating, he wiped his palms over his face.

On Friday, when he got up to preach at congregational prayers, he greeted people near him. When he climbed the pulpit he turned his face to the congregation and saluted them. When he preached, he leaned over his staff. His face flushed, his eyes reddened, he raised his voice. He appeared wrathful, as if he were warning about imminent danger from an army, or as if he were ordering an army to attack the enemy. He would say, "Your night has turned into day!" When he spoke to his warriors during battle, he leaned over his sword.

When revelations came to him, he would bow his head low, as if a heavy load were on his neck. He would appear crushed. Once he received a revelation while mounted on a camel: the knees of the camel gave out. Even when it was cold, drops of sweat like pearls would roll down his forehead. The color of his face would change; a strange sound like the buzzing of many bees would emanate from around his face. He would have terrible headaches. They would put henna on his head to alleviate the pain.

His Passing

He left this world at the age of sixty-three, in the city of Medina, to which he had migrated ten years earlier. His last words were *jalâlu rabbîr-rafi'. Faqad ballaght* (The sublime majesty of my Lord! For I have fulfilled my mission) and then he gave up his blessed soul.

His last advice to us was:

Do not ever abandon prayer. Do not ever abandon prayer. Do not ever abandon prayer. And fear Allah in your treatment of those under your control.

♦

May the true and intended meaning of these words find its place in your hearts. May they paint an image in your hearts' eye that is of the best shape and form imaginable. May you feel as close to that image as a child to the most beneficent of fathers.

Yet this intimacy should not make us suppose that he is like us. Is a chip of stone the same as a diamond, even though they are both rocks? Are the sun and a candle the same because they both shed light?

May we see his real shape in this life, when our souls become light and soar to the heavens in our dreams. In following his path, in imitating his character, may we be worthy to gather under his banner on the Day of Judgment. May we receive the intercession of the one whom Allah sent as His mercy upon the universe. May we be blessed to love him and Allah more than everything else. May we find Allah's pleasure and grace and enter Paradise.

All blessings and salutations of Allah be upon His beloved Prophet Muhammad whose soul He has created from the divine light of His essence, whom He has made a mirror of His beautiful attributes, and whom He has sent as His mercy. And peace and blessings be upon the members of his household, his family and descendants, and his companions and helpers, and the saints of all times who carry his light.༄

THE NAMES OF
THE PROPHET

O ALLAH, for as long as day turns to night and night recedes into day, for as long as the ages succeed one another, as day and night unceasingly follow upon each other and as the glowing stars remain suspended in the firmament, we beg that You bestow Your grace and favors upon our Master Muhammad and that You transmit unto his blessed soul and unto the souls of the people of his house our greetings and our respect, and that You bestow upon him Your peace and blessings in great abundance.

So may Allah bestow His peace and blessings upon our Master Muhammad and upon all the prophets and messengers; upon the saints and the righteous servants; upon the angels and upon those who reside by the Throne of Grace; and upon the obedient and vigilant servants among the people of the earth and those of the skies. And may Allah Most High be pleased with His Prophet and with all His companions and people. *Âmin.*

Muhammad, peace and blessings be upon him, is the one who is

sent as a mercy upon the universe
(Surah Anbiya', 107)

The light of his soul was the first creation to issue from the Light of Allah, and everything else is created from his light. He said, "O Jabir, the first creation that Allah created is the soul of your prophet." When he was asked at what point he became a prophet, he answered, "I was a prophet when Adam was between water and clay." He said, "Whoever sees me sees the truth."

Allah says:

And whoever obeys Allah and His Messenger, He will cause him to enter gardens wherein rivers flow.

(Surah Fath, 17)

And he has said, "As long as you do not love me more than anything else you have, your faith is not complete." For Allah says:

Certainly a Messenger has come to you from amongst yourselves; grievous to him is your falling into distress; most solicitous for you; to the believers he is merciful.

(Surah Tawbah, 128)

He upon whom Allah has bestowed

... a tremendous nature

(Surah Qalam, 4)

is sent to teach us to be noble in behavior, morals, and character. "Whoever prays to Allah to bestow upon His Messenger His peace and blessings, receives Allah's blessings tenfold, and may hope for the intercession of His Prophet on the Day of Judgment, and to enter Paradise."

We are presenting 201 beautiful names of our beloved Prophet as mentioned in the *Dalâ'il al-Khayrat* (1533 CE) of Shaykh 'Imran az-Zannati, may his soul be sanctified. Allah praises His Prophet with most of these names in the Holy Qur'an, and announces his coming by certain names in the other Holy Books: the Torah, the Zabur (Psalms of David), and the Gospel. They also appear in the Hadith, or traditions of the Prophet.

Shaykh Ibn al-Faris reports from Hadrat Ibn al-'Arabi that he had counted 2,020 beautiful attributes of our Prophet. Imam al-Kastalani, the author of the interpretation of the great hadith collection *Bukhari al-Sharif*, has counted 1,000 beautiful names.

May the ones who read the beautiful names of the Beloved of Allah contemplate the meaning, properties, and effects of these names and feel the love, the respect, and the consideration with which we hope their hearts will be inspired. We must realize that to love is not within our will, but within the greater will of Allah. He is the one who inspires the heart with love. By ourselves we cannot love Allah and His Prophet; by ourselves a man cannot even love a woman, or a woman, a man. In Islam it is unlawful for a man to insist that his wife love him or for a wife to insist upon the affection of her husband, for that is considered equivalent to forcing someone to lie. As a person cannot be forced to love, and we cannot force ourselves to love someone, how then should we understand the hadith, "If you do not love me more than anything else you have, your faith is not complete?" First comes the wish to love him, which can only be obtained through knowing him, through knowing his beautiful names, through finding a trace of these attributes in our own selves, through praying for him and for his blessings, through following his path and his example. Then, if Allah wills, you will be blessed with His love, and in return, you will love Him and find Paradise in this world and in the Hereafter.

His being was of light; he had no shadow. His beautiful face shone like the sun and radiated light around him. At night people saw by this light. It is written in the Holy Qur'an that in the darkness of the Day of Judgment the light of faith of the believers will illuminate the space around them, and the hypocrites, envious, will come close to them to profit from this light.

Allah, addressing His Beloved, whose name is written with His upon the firmament as *Lâ ilâha ill' Allâh, Muhammad rasulu Llâh* (There is no god worthy of worship except Allah, and Muhammad is His Messenger) says: "If it were not for you, I would not have created the creation." Therefore the greatest gift bestowed by Allah upon the universe is His Beloved. He says in the Holy Qur'an:

> *And if you count Allah's favors, you will not be able to number them.*

(Surah Ibrahim, 34)

Thus if we try to count the beautiful attributes of our beloved Prophet, the best of Allah's favors, we will be unable to number them.

1. *Muhammad* The most praised one.

He is praised upon earth and in the heavens, from the beginning to the end, by men and *jinn* and angels, rocks and trees and animals, by prophets before him since Adam, by saints until Doomsday. As all of this cannot give him due praise, we beg Allah to praise him. He is the only one who truly knows the value and the mystery of His Muhammad, peace and blessings be upon him, and He is the only one who can truly praise him.

2. *Ahmad* The most praiseworthy of those who praise Allah.

This is the celestial name of the Prophet. Allah, the Ever-Existing, the All-Powerful, created a sacred light from His divine light 360,000 years before He created the rest of creation. That light upon light praised Allah before and during the creation of heaven and the heavenly and earth and the earthly. The inhabitants of the heavens named that light Ahmad. As his praise of Allah is greater than the praise of all that is created, he is called *ahmad al-hamidin* (the greatest of givers of praise).

Ahmad is the name by which he is mentioned in the Gospel.

> *And when Jesus son of Mary said, "O Children of Israel, surely I am the Messenger of Allah to you, verifying that which is before me of the Torah and giving good news of a Messenger who will come after me, his name being Ahmad..."*
>
> (Surah Saff, 6)

> In the Bible, Jesus, peace be upon him, says: I have yet many things to say unto you, but ye cannot bear them now. Howbeit when he, the Spirit of Truth, is come, he will guide you unto all truth, for he shall not speak of himself, but whatsoever he shall hear, that shall he speak; and he will show you things to come. He shall glorify me. (John 14:17)

That Spirit of Truth who speaks only Allah's words is Ahmad.

3. *Hamîd* The only one who is given the ability to praise and give thanks to Allah.

He is the one who will praise Allah on the Day of Judgment, just as he praised Allah as the first created light. On that Day he will put his blessed face on the ground in prostration, praise the Lord, and beg mercy for us. *Hamîd* says, On that day my Lord will enable me to praise Him as I never did before, and I will praise Him more than I ever did before. Then He will tell me, "Lift your head, My Beloved. I promised that

> *I will give to thee so that thou wilt be well pleased.*
>
> (Surah Duha, 5)

and I accept your intercession for your people until you are satisfied. Your praises are accepted, your intercession is accepted."

4. *Mahmûd* The praised one.

He is praised by all who are raised on the Day of Judgment, for he will be the only one who will intercede for the faithful and whose intercession will be valid. He is the one who has been raised to the station of great glory—al-maqâm al-mahmûd. Allah asked His Beloved:

> *During a part of the night keep awake and pray, beyond what is incumbent on thee. Maybe thy Lord will raise thee to maqâman mahmûdan (a station of glory).*
>
> (Surah Bani Isra'il, 79)

Mahmûd is the name with which he is mentioned in the Psalms of David.

5. *Âhid* The only one who will protect his people from Hellfire.

On the day when sinners will be thrown into Hellfire, Allah will address *Âhid* and say, "O My Beloved, these are the ones who have denied Us and revolted against Us because they have denied you, disobeyed you, and not followed you. You can use the Hellfire as you wish upon them. And these are the ones who said they believed in and obeyed you, but succumbed to the temptation of the accursed Devil and the desires of their flesh, and sinned. You can use My Hellfire upon them or free them." He is the key that locks the seven doors of Hell, he is the key that opens the eight doors of Paradise; he is the mercy of Allah upon the universe.

When Allah willed to take His Beloved to Himself, He sent the angel Gabriel, peace be upon him, who said, "Allah Most High asks you: When He takes your soul, where in His Paradise do you wish your body to rest?"

At this the heavens, in great pride and joy, declared, "The suns are within us, the moons and the stars are within us, the Throne and Canopy and the Celestial Ka'bah in the seventh heaven and Paradise are within us, and Muhammad will be within us!"

The Mercy Upon the Universe asked, "O my brother Gabriel, where will my people be buried?"

Gabriel answered, "Surely under this earth, O Messenger of Allah."

The Beloved of Allah said, "In that case, I ask to be buried here with them, so that I will be with them when we are raised."

Then this world with joy declared, "O heavens!

The suns the moons, the stars, the Throne, the Ka'bah of the seventh heaven, and Paradise may be within you, but the Beloved of Allah is within me!"

6. *Wâhid* The unique one.

He is unique among men. He has come among us as a human being like ourselves, most beautiful in form and character, the gentlest, the highest in knowledge and wisdom. But his uniqueness is in the station bestowed upon him by the Creator. As Allah imbued Adam with the knowledge of all the Names, so He gave the Last of the Prophets the knowledge of all the Names, all the Attributes, and the Essence. These he had received at the first creation of his light. He saw them with his own eyes upon his Ascension. He saw even his Lord, who is free of all dimensions.

7. *Mâhî* The annihilator of the darkness of faithless and heedlessness.

He is the one who came to a world immersed in darkness, filled with tyranny, idolatry, denial, depravity, and disorder. He was sent as the mercy of the Creator upon the whole universe, and with the light of his message the tyranny turned into peace, the darkness into light, denial into faith, depravity into purity, and disorder into harmony. With his teaching, the darkness and depravity were annihilated and the world was enlightened with the light of faith, knowledge, and wisdom. The sins and revolts of the believers disappeared with the love, respect, and obedience that he inspired for Allah and for himself, and the love and care which he inspired in human beings for one another.

8. *Hâshir* The gatherer, the unifier, under whom all will reassemble here and on the Day of Judgment.

He is the one who foretold that all people—who are all created Muslims, submissive to Allah, but then with their worldly environment assume false identities—will soon realize and gather under one God and the final message brought by His Messenger. On the Day of Judgment, also, all believers will gather around him under the shade of his banner of grace, hoping for his intercession.

9. *'Âqib* The successor of all the prophets; the final prophet.

Allah says:

Muhammad...is the Messenger of Allah and the Seal of the prophets...

(Surah Ahzab, 40)

No other Messenger will come after him until Doomsday, as his message will stay intact and unchanged until the end of time. He is called *'Aqib* because the totality of good character, morals, and deeds is complete within him. Neither the degree of perfection of other human beings nor their closeness to their Creator can ever surpass his.

This name will be remembered and mentioned by the inhabitants of Hell, as the sinners among his followers will be thrown into Hell, and after their punishment, their state will be made known to him. Then he will intercede and beg for mercy for them. When he does so, that place in Hell where the Muslims met their temporary punishment will lose its fire and be closed.

211

10. **Tâ Hâ** The pure purifier and the guide to true faith.

Ta Ha is the name of a chapter of the Holy Qur'an and one of the Names of Allah. Allah honors His Beloved Prophet by some of His own names and attributes.

The ones who know say that the letters "T" and "A" of Ta stand for *Tahir*, the pure and purified. The letter "H" and "A" of Ha stand for *Hadi*, the guide. He is the pure one who has helped purify humanity from faithlessness, sin, and error, and who has led us from heedlessness and ignorance into the straight path to the truth.

"T" also stands for *tuba* of *tûba li-man hudiya bihi* (blessings upon those who have been guided by him), while "H" stands for *Hâdî*, (the guide). Good tidings to those who have found the true path to Allah's pleasure and Paradise through believing in, loving, and obeying the Messenger of Allah.

In the system that assigns numerical values to Arabic letters, "T" equals 9 and "H" equals 5, totaling 14, the number of the day of the lunar cycle when the moon is full. This indicates that his light is like the full moon, eliminating the darkness of unconsciousness, faithlessness, and ignorance.

11. **Yâ Sîn** The Perfect Man, who is master of all humanity.

Yâ Sîn is the name of a chapter in the Qur'an that is considered to be the heart of the Holy Book. It is also one of the Names of Allah. It is said that the letters "Y" and "S" stand for *yâ insân* (O Human Being), the best of all human beings, past, present, and future. It also means the master of all humanity. Allah has given him a name from among His own Names because the truth of Muhammad , peace and blessings be upon him, can be truly known to Him alone.

12. **Tâhir** Pure and clean.

He is not only cleansed from moral and spiritual stains but also from material dirt. He is clean in this world and in the other—in his faith, in his worship, in everything he did, in everything he said. His breath, his spittle, his blood were pure. At the battle of Uhud, when his blessed cheek was wounded, Malik ibn Sinan (may Allah be pleased with him), one of the Companions, pressed his mouth to the wound and swallowed the blood. The Prophet did not stop him from doing this, but said, "O Malik, that blood you swallowed will bring you health in this world, and will protect you against Hellfire in the Hereafter."

13. **Mutahhar** The one who is rendered pure by Allah.

As *Mutahhar*, he purifies those who follow him from disbelief, sin, the dirt of the world and the desires of the flesh. He polishes them with the light of Allah's unity and perfumes them with the love of their Lord and their Prophet. On the Day of Judgment he will cleanse us of all the afflictions of this world and the Hereafter, and save us from purification by Hellfire.

14. **Tayyib** The pleasant and beautifully fragrant one.

His blessed body smelled more beautiful than the pink roses of May. When he caressed the head of a child or held someone's hand, his fragrance remained for a long time. People knew where he had passed because his fragrance lingered in the air. His wives put his perspiration upon themselves as the best of perfumes.

15. *Sayyîd* The Prince of the Universe, the highest of the prophets.

Many among the wise have interpreted this name in different ways.

"*Sayyîd* is he who is gracious in the opinion of Allah." ('Abdullah ibn 'Abbas)

"*Sayyîd* is he whose worship is complete, who is pious and chaste, who does not take revenge against injustice and tyranny but forgives, who deals gently even with his enemies." (Qatadah)

"*Sayyîd* is he whose state is equal, whether he is pleased or angry." ('Ikrimah)

The Prophet himself has said, "I am the *sayyîd*, master, of all men on the Day of Judgment," as Allah calls Himself

> *mâliki yawm ad-dîn* (I am the Owner, the Judge on the Day of Judgment.)
>
> (Surah Fatihah, 3)

Can you think of the awe and dread of that Day whose judge is Allah, and the grandeur and majesty of the one who is master of all humanity on that day? On that day, when all people are raised, when a thousand feet will stand on one foot, when men are trembling with fear, immersed in their own sweat, brains boiling in their skulls, all hoping for each others' aid, mothers, fathers, priests, popes, saints, even all the prophets thinking of their own salvation, and unable to help. The Beloved of Allah, the Master of the Day of Judgment, will be the only one to turn to for help.

16. **Rasûl** The Messenger of Allah.

Allah says:

> *Certainly you have in the Messenger of Allah*
> *an excellent example.*
>
> (Surah Ahzab, 26)

17. **Nabî** The Prophet who speaks Allah's words.

Allah describes His Prophet Muhammad, saying,

> *O Prophet, surely We have sent thee as a wit-*
> *ness and a bearer of good news and a warner.*
> *And as an inviter to Allah by His permission,*
> *and as a light-giving lamp.*
>
> (Surah Ahzab, 45-46)

18. **Rasûl ar-rahmah** The Messenger of the Most Compassionate.

Allah the Merciful, the Forgiver, addresses us through His Messenger:

> *Say: O My servants who have transgressed*
> *against their souls, despair not of the mercy of*
> *Allah, for Allah forgives all sins. For He is the*
> *Oft-Forgiving, Most Merciful.*
>
> (Surah Zumar, 53)

And Allah also says of His Prophet:

> *And We sent thee not but as a mercy upon the*
> *universe.*
>
> (Surah Anbiya', 107)

Allah does not punish the sins of the believers, and delays the punishment also of the nonbeliever until his death, for the sake of this Messenger whom He has sent as

His mercy upon the whole of creation.

19. *Qayyim* The right and good one who loves and is generous to all people.

He also teaches his followers brotherhood and love for each other, gives to them, and teaches them to give to each other what is needed in this world and in the Hereafter.

20. *Jâmi'* The one in whom all knowledge is gathered.

Allah taught Hadrat Adam, peace be upon him, all the words, and the names of all that exists from the beginning to the end, and He taught Hadrat Ibrahim, peace be upon him, all the attributes. In His last prophet He gathered all the knowledge of all the Names, all the attributes, and the Essence. Muhammad, peace and blessings be upon him, not only knew them, but saw them and lived them during his ascension in the Night Journey, when he visited all the heavens, met the souls of all the prophets, saw the hundred levels of eight Paradises and seven hells, and spoke 90,000 words with his Lord.

21. *Muqtafî* The last one, who follows and contains all the prophets.

The Last of the Prophets has said:

The resemblance between me and the other prophets is like a beautiful house which is complete except for a last brick. All who see this marvel at its beauty, but are also shocked by the missing brick. With me, that building of prophethood is completed.

216

He is the mercy upon the universe. Allah has wished to seal His messages with a Messenger who is His Mercy. Allah has honored the followers of His last prophet by making them the last community, so that their sins and errors are hidden from the previous Messengers. Allah has made their punishment light, His rewards for them greater, and their time of waiting until the Day of Judgment shorter.

22. *Muqaffi* The one behind whom are all the other prophets, who follow him and are confirmed in him.

The Blessed Prophet has said:

> Allah Most High has honored me to be at the head of all. No prophet has reached to my level of closeness with Allah. They are all behind me, and they all follow me in all their natural and spiritual actions and merits in this world and in the Hereafter.

23. *Rasûl al-malâhim* Messenger to the warriors of truth.

Those who are honored to follow the most merciful, compassionate, and gentlest of prophets are the fiercest warriors against the tyranny of the unfaithful over the faithful. This *jihad* is ordered by Allah and helped by Allah. One of the miracles of Islam is the repeated victory of a handful of Muslim warriors during the short period of 25 years over the then greatest powers of the world, the Sassanids of Persia and the Byzantines.

Within the first 40 years of the Islamic era, the whole of the Arabian Peninsula, Egypt and North Africa,

Persia and Asia Minor, and the Caucasus were in Muslim hands.

That which rendered the believers victorious was Allah's help and their faith in Him. But the Prophet has said that the greater battle is the war with one's own ego and one's own Devil, and the greatest victory is won over one's own faithlessness.

24. *Rasûl ar-râhah* The Messenger of appeasement and quietude.

25. *Kamîl* The perfect one.

26. *Iklîl* The crown of the believers.

27. *Muddaththir* The one who shows patience towards those who tyrannize him.

Because he was patient toward those who were hostile, he has been addressed in the Qur'an as:

> *O thou wrapped up [in a mantle]...for thy Lord's cause be patient and constant.*
>
> (Surah Muddaththir, 1,7)

28. *Muzammil* The one who wraps himself up in his cloak as he did in the awe of the first revelation.

29. *Abdullâh* Allah's ultimate servant.

With this name he received the highest honor, as to be the true servant of Allah is the highest level to which any human being may aspire.

30. *Habîbullâh* The Beloved of Allah.

218

This name is proper only to him.

31. *Safiyullâh* The chosen of Allah out of the whole creation.

He was purified, sustained, brought up, and educated by Allah Himself. From him all that is lacking was taken away, and to him all perfection was given.

32. *Najî'ullâh* The deliverer who leads to salvation.

33. *Kalîmullâh* The one who converses with Allah.

He spoke 90,000 words with Allah in his ascension during the Night Journey.

34. *Khâtim al-anbiyâ'* The Seal of the Prophets, with whom all prophethood is fulfilled.

Allah declares:

> *Muhammad...is the apostle of Allah and the seal of the prophets.*
> (Surah Ahzab, 40)

35. *Khâtim ar-rusul* The Seal of the Messengers.

36. *Muhyî* The vivifier of dead hearts with the light of faith.

37. *Munjî* The one who delivers from sin.

38. *Mudhakkir* The one who reminds us of the Creator and of the Day of Judgment.

39. *Nâsir* The helper of humanity, the ally of the righteous.

40. *Mansûr* The one made triumphant in this world and in the Hereafter.

He is the one fortified by the assistance of Gabriel and other angels, and by Allah Himself.

41. *Nabî ar-rahmah* The prophet who was sent as Allah's mercy upon the universe.

42. *Nabî at-tawbah* The prophet of repentance, striving for human welfare.

43. *Harîs 'alaykum* The one filled with solicitude for you.

Mentioned in the Qur'an as the one zealous for your salvation. Allah says:

It grieves him that ye should perish;
ardently anxious is he over you; to the believ-
ers is he most kind and merciful.

(Surah Tawbah, 128)

44. *Ma'lûm* The well known.

45. *Shâhir* The celebrated one.

46. *Shâhid* The witness.

47. *Shahîd* The martyr.

48. *Mashshûd* The witnessed.

49. **Bashîr** The sender of good news to the believers.

50. **Mubashshir** The bringer of good news of blessings and Paradise.

51. **Nazîr** The one who calls humanity to virtue with warnings of Allah's wrath.

52. **Munzir** The one who warns and dissuades from sin.

53. **Nûr** The sacred light.

54. **Sirâj** The torch of the right path.
        The one illuminated with the light of faith and Islam.

55. **Misbah** The lamp that contains the light of faith and Islam which lights the realms of worship, submission, and salvation.

56. **Hudâ** The guidance to Truth and Paradise.

57. **Mahdî** The rightly guided one, guide to the path of knowledge, obedience, and worship.

58. **Munîr** The illuminator of the universe.

59. **Dâ'î** The one who calls to faith and Islam.

60. **Mad'û** The one who heard and accepted the divine call.

61. *Mujîb* The one who accepts prayers.

He brought humanity Allah's ordinances and warned us against sins. He became an example of acting in accordance with divine teaching, and he interceded for the good and the sinner alike.

62. *Mujâb* The answered one, the answer to our prayers.

63. *Hâfî* The true answerer of all questions.

64. *'Afû* The clement.

He is the example of forgiving the wrong done to him; Allah forgives the one who forgives.

65. *Walî* The friend of Allah and of all who believe.

66. *Haqq* The Truth.

67. *Qawî* The powerful.

68. *Amin* The trustworthy.

He was called Muhammad *al-amin* (Muhammad the Trustworthy) by the Meccans before he received the divine order to declare his prophethood at the age of 40.

69. *Ma'mûn* The one in whom people confide.

70. *Karîm* The generous one.

Allah bestows upon him the attribute of one of his beautiful names, the All-Generous One.

71. *Mukarram* The ennobled one.

72. *Makîn* The authoritative one.

73. *Matîn* The firm and consistent one.

74. *Mubîn* The distinguisher and the explainer.

75. *Mu'ammil* The hopeful one.

76. *Wasûl* The uniter.

77. *Dhû quwwah* The source of strength.

78. *Dhû hurmah* The source of sacredness.

79. *Dhû makanah* The source of integrity.

80. *Dhû 'izz* The source of might.

81. *Dhû fadl* The source of virtue.

82. *Mutâ'* The one whom the faithful obey.

83. *Mutî'* The one who is obedient to Allah.

84. *Qidâm as-sidq* The one constantly sincere.

85. *Rahmah* Compassion.

86. *Bushrâ* Good news.

87. *Ghawth* Savior.

88. *Ghayth* The benevolent one who brings dead hearts to life just as rain gives life to the earth.

89. *Ghiyâth* The helper.

90. *Ni'matullâh* The blessing of Allah.

91. *Hadiyatullâh* The gift of Allah to the universe.

92. *'Urwah wuthqâ* The firm tie that binds humanity to its Creator.

93. *Sirâtullâh* The path leading to Allah and the Truth.

94. *Sirât mustaqîm* The straight and shortest way leading to Allah.

95. *Dhikrullâh* The remembrance of Allah.

96. *Sayfullâh* The sword of Allah.

97. *Hizbullâh* Allah's partisan, destroyer of the enemies of Allah.

98. *An-najm al-thaqîb* The Star whose fire burns Devils.

99. *Mustafâ* The divinely elected.

100. *Mujtabâ* The chosen one.

101. *Muntaqâ* The one chosen for his purity.

102. *Ummî* The unlettered one who has no teacher among men, who is divinely taught.

103. *Mukhtar* The chosen one who is autonomous.

104. *Âjir* The reward of the believers.

105. *Jabbâr* The all-compelling one.

106. *Abul-Qâsim* The father of Qasim.

107. *Abu Tâhir* The father of Tahir.

108. *Abu Tayyib* The father of Tayyib.

109. *Abu Ibrahîm* The father of Ibrahim.

110. *Mushaffa'* The one given the right of intercession.

111. *Shâfi'* The intercessor.

112. *Sâlih* The righteous.

113. *Muslih* The conciliator.

114. *Muhaymin* The protector and guardian.

115. *Sâdiq* The truthful.

116. *Musaddaq* The one proved true by the Truth that comes through him.

117. **Sidq** The essence of truthfulness.

118. **Sayyid al-mursalîn** The master and best of all Messengers.

119. **Imâm al-muttaqîn** The leader of the pious who fear Allah.

120. **Qâ'id al-ghurri al-muhajjalîn** Protector and guide of the believers.

121. **Khalîl ar-Rahmân** The close friend of the All-Merciful Allah.

122. **Barr** The good and beneficent one.

123. **Mabarr** The essence of piety and beneficence.

124. **Wajîh** The one distinguished from all else.

125. **Nasîh** The true counselor.

126. **Nasîh** Transformer of men's souls.

127. **Wakîl** The faithful trustee.

128. **Mutawakkil** The one who puts all his trust in Allah.

129. **Kafîl** The guarantor.

130. **Shafîq** The compassionate, kind, and benevolent one.

131. *Muqîm as-sunnah* The one who holds the ordinances of Allah.

132. *Muqaddas* The sanctified one.

133. *Ruh al-quddûs* Essence of the divine.

134. *Ruh al-haqq* The essence of truth.

135. *Ruh al-qist* The essence of justice.

136. *Kafî* The one who suffices for the believers.

137. *Muktafî* The one sufficient unto himself.

138. *Baligh* The one who has arrived at spiritual perfection.

139. *Muballigh* The bearer of news.

140. *Shafî* The curer of sick hearts.

141. *Wasîl* The one who has attained the divine.

142. *Mawsul* The one who has been attained.

143. *Sâbiq* The one who precedes everything.

144. *Sâ'iq* The impelling motive for the faith of the faithful.

145. *Hâdî* The guide.

146. *Muhdî* The one who gives guidance.

147. *Muqaddam* The premise of Islam.

148. *'Azîz* The highly esteemed beloved with no equal among men.

149. *Fadîl* The one superior in virtue and generosity.

150. *Mufaddal* The favored of Allah made superior to all beings.

151. *Fâtih* The conqueror of hearts, who opens them to faith and truth.

152. *Miftah* The key that opens the doors of Paradise and locks the doors of Hell.

153. *Miftah ar-rahmah* The key to Allah's mercy.

154. *Miftah al-jannah* The key of Paradise.

155. *'Alam al-imân* The symbol of faith that leads one to faith.

156. *'Alam al-yaqîn* The symbol of certitude that leads one to certitude.

157. *Dalîl al-khayrât* The guide to good deeds.

158. *Musahhih al-hasanât* The one who renders the wrong, right and the ugly, beautiful.

159. *Muqîl al-atharât* The foreseer and warner of errors.

160. *Safûh'an az-zallât* The one who deters errors.

161. *Sâhib ash-shafâ'ah* The one endowed with intercession.

162. *Sâhib al-makân* The one imbued with the highest degree of morals and character.

163. *Sâhib al-qidâm* The one endued with the highest station.

164. *Makhsûs bil-'izz* The one to whom all might and honor are proper.

165. *Makhsûs bil-majd* The one to whom all that is noble, sublime, and majestic is proper.

166. *Makhsûs bish-sharaf* The one to whom all excellence is proper.

167. *Sâhib al-wasîlah* The possessor of the means to Allah's mercy.

168. *Sâhib as-sayf* The owner of the sword against Allah's enemies.

169. *Sâhib al-fadîlah* The source of Allah's grace.

170. *Sâhib al-izâr* The owner of the cloak of prophet-

hood who is mentioned by this name in holy books.

171. *Sâhib al-hujjah* The possessor of the proof.

172. *Sâhib as-sultân* The owner of the sovereignty of kings.

173. *Sâhib al-ridâ'* The owner of the woolen cloak.

174. *Sâhib ad-darajât ar-râfi'ah* The one endowed with the exalted station.

175. *Sâhib at-taj* The crowned one, crowned with the crown of Paradise on the night of his Ascension.

176. *Sâhib al-mighfar* The one who wears the helmet of the holy knight.

177. *Sâhib al-liwâ'* Holder of the Banner of Praise under which all prophets and believers will gather on the Day of Judgment.

178. *Sâhib al-mi'râj* The master of ascension who was brought, during his lifetime, above the seven heavens, to the divine realms close to Allah.

179. *Sâhib al-qadîb* The holder of the rod with which he broke the 360 idols around the Ka'bah on the day of the conquest of Mecca.

180. *Sâhib al-Burâq* The rider of *Buraq*, the heavenly carrier which brought him from the city of Mecca to

Jerusalem on the night of the Ascension.

181. *Sâhib al-khatam* The carrier of the Seal of Prophethood, which was between his shoulder blades.

182. *Sâhib al-'alâmah* The one endowed with the distinct signs of prophethood.

183. *Sâhib al-burhân* The one endowed with the miracles proving his prophethood.

184. *Sâhib al-bayân* The one endowed with the greatest expression of prophethood, which is the Holy Qur'an.

185. *Fâsih al-lisân* The one whose speech is rendered most eloquent and effective.

186. *Mutahhir al-janân* The source of knowledge, wisdom, and gentleness, whose heart is purified and who purifies hearts.

187. *Ra'ûf* The clement one on whom Allah has bestowed His own Name, by which he is mentioned in the Qur'an.

188. *Rahîm* The merciful one, upon whom Allah the Most Merciful bestowed His own Name.

189. *Udhn khayr* The hearer of good.

190. *Sahîh al-Islâm* The truth of Islam which corrects and cancels human distortions of divine truths previously revealed, and reestablishes the true message of Allah.

191. *Sayyîd al-kawnayn* The master of all created beings in this world and the Hereafter.

192. *'Ayn an-na'îm* The source through which Allah's blessings come in this world and the Hereafter.

193. *'Ayn al-qurr* The source of light and splendor.

194. *Sa'd Allâh* The joy of Allah who as the first created intelligence, contains the salvation, the victory, peace, and blessing of all creation.

195. *Sa'd al-khalq* The joy of all created beings, being the best and the most generous and closest to Allah among them.

196. *Khâtib al-umâm* The preacher to humanity.

197. *'Alam al-hudâ* The sign of guidance to truth, Allah's pleasure, and Paradise.

198. *Kâshif al-karb* The one who lifts the pain, afflictions, and difficulties from humanity.

199. *Râfi' al-rutab* The one who raises the levels of those who believe and obey him.

200. *'Izz al-a'râb* The glory of the Arabs.

201. *Sâhib al-faraj* The source of consolation, who gives bliss and comfort to those who believe in his prophethood and follow his commands.

THE STORY OF THE VISIT OF THE DEVIL, THE ACCURSED

Mu'adh ibn Jabal relates from Hadrat Ibn 'Abbas (may Allah be pleased with them):

ONE DAY, at the home of one of the Companions, a congregation was gathered around the Prophet. In the middle of a wonderful discourse, an ugly voice from the outside was heard. "O people inside, would you permit me to enter? I have business with you!" it said.

Everyone looked at the Prophet. He said to the ones present, "Do you recognize the owner of this voice?"

The Companions answered, "Allah and His Messenger know best."

The Prophet said, "It is Satan the Accursed."

On hearing that, Hadrat 'Umar (may Allah be pleased with him), who was present, drew his sword. "O Messenger of Allah, permit me to go and cut off his head!" he said.

The Prophet replied, "No, 'Umar, don't you know that you cannot kill him? He has permission to exist until Doomsday." Then he added, "Open the door and admit him, as he did not come on his own but on Allah's orders. Listen to what he says, and try to understand."

Then Rawi (may Allah be pleased with him) one of the Companions, continues the tale:

They opened the door, and he appeared in front of

233

us as an old man, cross-eyed [or blind in one eye] and scant of beard, with only six or seven long hairs hanging from his chin. He had a very big head, his crossed eyes close to the top of his head, high on his forehead, with big thick hanging lips like those of a water buffalo. He saluted the Prophet and the Companions, to which the Prophet responded, "O Accursed, the *salâm* and salutations belong to Allah Most High." Then he said, "I heard you are here on business. What is it?"

Satan said: "I did not wish to come here, I was forced to. An angel came to me from your Lord, who honors whom He wishes, and said, 'Allah Most High orders you to go to Muhammad, but you will go to him in humility and abasement, and be submissive and tractable. You will tell him how you seduce and mislead humankind. You are going to answer all his questions truthfully, without a single lie.' And Allah said that if I lied to you He would turn me into ashes and blow me away in the wind, and my enemies would laugh at me. I come with such orders, O Muhammad."

Then the Prophet asked the Devil, "Tell me, who in the creation do you hate most?"

The Devil answered, "You, O Muhammad! There is no one in the whole creation that I hate more. There is none other like you."

The Messenger of Allah, peace and blessings be upon him, confirmed that the Devil was his own and all the prophets' greatest foe. He asked, "Whom else do you detest, besides me?"

Satan said, "The young ones who have given up their pleasures and themselves for Allah's sake; the people of knowledge who act upon their knowledge and who decline all that is doubtful; and the ones who are clean, so clean that they wash three times that which they wish to cleanse. After that the patient poor, who neither ask from others the things they need, nor complain. After that the thankful rich, who give alms lawfully and spend lawfully." [Hadrat Anas lists fourteen enemies after the prophets: the knowledgeable who act on what they know; readers of the Qur'an who pattern themselves on it; those who call to prayer for Allah's sake; the satisfied poor; the compassionate; the generous; those who perform the morning prayer on time; advisors and reformers; abstainers from unlawful food and sexual relations; those who are always in ablution; the modest; those who place their trust in Allah; benefiters of the poor; the devout who are busy in Allah's service.]

Then the Prophet asked: "What happens to you, O Accursed One, when my people perform their prayers?"

"I shake and tremble as if stricken with malaria because I see your people raised in blessing and power each time they prostrate."

"What happens to you, O Accursed, when my people fast?"

"I have my hands and feet tied until they break their fast."

"What happens when they all meet on the Pilgrimage at the house of their Lord?"

"I lose my wits, I go mad."

"What happens to you when they recite the Holy Qur'an?"

"I melt like lead turning to hot liquid in the fire."

"And when they pay alms?"

"I am torn to pieces, as if the generous donor took a

saw and sawed me into four pieces, because there are four blessings that the donor receives—the blessing of abundance, love and respect from Allah's creatures, a shield from Hellfire, and relief from distress and troubles."

Then the Messenger of Allah asked the Devil what he thought of his beloved Companions. About Hadrat Abu Bakr he said, "I hate him. Even before Islam he refused to obey, nay, even to hear me. How can he now listen to me?" About Hadrat 'Umar ibn al-Khattab he said, "I run away whenever I see him!" About Hadrat 'Uthman ibn 'Affan he said, "I am ashamed in front of him. Even the angels of mercy are ashamed in front of him." And about Hadrat 'Ali ibn Abi Talib he said, "Oh, if I could just be safe from him, if he would just let me be, I would let him be. But he will not leave me alone!"

Having heard the answers of the accursed Satan, the Prophet thanked Allah and said, "Praise be to Allah who has blessed my people with such felicity and cursed you with such negativity until that appointed time."

When the Devil heard that, he said, "Alas, alas for you, what felicity for your people? How can you feel there is safety for them as long as I exist? I enter their very veins, their very flesh, and they cannot even suspect, let alone see or feel me. I swear by Allah who has given me time until Doomsday that I will seduce them all, the intelligent and the simple-minded, the learned as well as the ignorant, the devout as well as the sinner. None will be safe from me except the true servants of Allah."

The Prophet asked, "Who are the true servants of Allah, according to you?"

The Devil said, "You know well, O Muhammad, that whoever loves his money and his property Allah does not count among His servants. Whenever I see someone who does not say 'mine' and 'me,' who does not love either money or flattery, I know he is truly a servant of Allah and I run away from him. As long as a person loves money, property, flattery, he obeys me: he is my servant. I need many servants and I have many servants. I am not alone. I have 70,000 children, each of them with his assigned duties. Each of my 70,000 children has 70,000 satans serving under him, all assigned to different posts. Many are with the young, and the older women, and with the theologians and preachers and shaykhs. There are almost no differences of opinion between your young people and my devils, and your children play happily with my children. And some of the devout and some of the pious get along very well with my people! My devils lead the imagination of the pious from one height to another. Arrogant, they leave the sincerity of their devotions. Soon they fight with each other, and they don't even know what is happening to them. Then I whisper to them, 'Disbelieve!,' but when they disbelieve, I say

> *I am free of you. Surely I fear Allah, the Lord of the Worlds.*
>
> (Surah Hashr, 16)

Then the accursed Devil told how he profited from human habits that he liked. About lying he said, "Do you know, O Muhammad, that lying is from me, and that I am the first liar? Whoever lies is my best friend; whoever swears to the truth of his lie is my beloved. You know, O Muhammad, that I swore by Allah and lied to Adam and Eve. I swore to them both

237

Surely I am a sincere advisor to you.

(Surah 'Araf, 21)

"I also love rejection and gossip. They are my delightful fruits. I detest loving families. If they think of rejecting each other, separating from each other, and talk about divorce, even if just once, the marriage bond in Allah's view is dissolved. The wife will be unlawful to the husband. When they sleep together, they will be adulterers. If they have a child he will be a bastard. I love all that.

"O Muhammad, let me tell you about my friends who abandon prayers or delay them. When it is time for prayer I make them imagine that there is still time, that they are busy. They should enjoy what they are doing, they can always pray later! I hope they will die before doing their next prayer, and some of them do. Even when they do their prayers late, their devotions are thrown in their faces. If I cannot succeed myself, I send them a human satan who will prevent them from their devotions. If I don't succeed again, I enter into their prayers. I tell them, 'Look to the right, look to the left! Think of the past, plan your future!' And when they do, I caress their cheeks and kiss their foreheads and take the peace from their hearts. You know, O Muhammad, that the prayers of those whose attention is outside of them or who are imagining things that do not belong in the presence of Allah are also rejected and thrown in their faces.

"And if I am not successful in that, I order them to do their prayers fast; they look like hens picking at grain. If I still don't succeed, I follow them to the congregational prayers and put bridles on their heads. I pull, and lift their heads from the prostration before the *imam*, and I push their heads down before the *imam* touches his head to the ground, and I am overjoyed to remember that Allah will turn those unruly heads into donkeys' heads on the Day of Judgment. If I am still not successful, I try at least to make them crack their fingers while they are making prayers! Then they will be among those who offer me praise instead of Allah. Or at least I will blow into their noses and make them yawn: if they open their mouths, a little devil will enter into them through their mouths and increase their love and ambition for this world. The one who loves and is ambitious for this world becomes my soldier; he obeys me and does as he is ordered.

"O Muhammad, how can you hope and be serene about your people's salvation and felicity? I have a trap at every corner for them. I go to the poor and tell them, 'What has Allah done for you? Why do you pray to Him? Prayer is for those to whom He has given in abundance.' Then I go to those who are sick and tell them to stop praying, and remind them that even Allah said

There is no blame on the sick.

(Surah Nur, 61)

I hope that they will die having abandoned their prayers, so that Allah will meet them with anger in the Hereafter.

"O Muhammad, if I have told a single lie, may scorpions bite me, and ask from Allah that He turn me into ashes! O Muhammad, do not be sure of your people. I have already converted a sixth of them, who have left their religion."

Then the Messenger of Allah, peace and blessings

239

be upon him, asked, "O Accursed One, with whom do you most like to spend your time?"

"The usurer."

"And your best friend?"

"The adulterer."

"With whom do you share your bed?"

"The drunkard."

"Who are your guests?"

"The thieves."

"Who are your representatives?"

"The magicians and soothsayers."

"What pleases you most?"

"Divorce."

"Whom do you love most?"

"Those who abandon their Friday prayers; tyrants and oppressors; the arrogant; servile scholars who hide the truth for the benefit of tyrants; dishonest tradesmen; dealers in fraud; slanderers; those who stir up trouble among friends."

Then the Prophet asked, "What breaks your heart, O Accursed One?"

"The determination and the firm footsteps of those who march against the enemies of Allah for Allah's sake."

"What gives you pain?"

"The repentance of the penitent."

"What makes you grimace?"

"The alms given in secret."

"What makes your eyes blind?"

"The extra prayer in the middle of the night."

"What makes you bow your head?""

"Prayer done in congregation."

"O Satan, according to you, who are the happiest

among people?"

"The ones who purposefully abandon their prayers."

"And the best among people?"

"The misers."

"What prevents you from doing your job?"

"The gathering of people of knowledge and their discourses."

"How do you eat your food?"

"With my left hand and the tips of my fingers."

"When the sun is hot, where do you seek shade?"

"Under people's dirty fingernails."

"What did you ask from My Lord on the day you were rejected from His presence?"

"I had ten requests that were accorded."

"What were they, O Accursed One?"

"I asked Allah to make me a partner in the properties and children of the children of Adam. He gave that to me, and He said

> *And incite whom thou canst with thy voice, and collect against them thy horse and thy foot, and share with them in wealth and children, and promise them. And the Devil promises them only to deceive.*
>
> (Surah Bani Isra'il, 64)

"I eat from the meat of animals killed without invoking the name of Allah, and from the food bought with money gained through interest, injustice, and tyranny. I am the shareholder of the property whose owner does not take refuge in Allah from me. I am part father of the child that comes from intercourse performed without invoking the name of Allah. I am the traveling companion of whoever rides in a vehicle that goes to an unlawful destination.

"I asked Allah to give me a house, and He gave me the public baths. I asked Allah to give me a temple, and He gave me the marketplaces as my temple. I asked Allah to give me a book. He gave me the books of poetry as my book. I asked for a call to prayer, and He gave me dance music. I asked for someone to share my bed, and He gave me the drunkard. I asked Allah for helpers. Allah gave me those who believe in free will. I asked Allah to give me brothers and sisters, and Allah gave me the squanderers who spend their money on evil things. Allah said

> *Surely the squanderers are the Devil's*
> *brethren*

(Surah Bani Isra'il, 27)

"Then I asked Allah to be able to see the children of Adam while they are unable to see me, and He accorded that to me. I wished that the very veins of the children of Adam be my routes, and it was given to me. So I flow in their veins as I wish, and I enter their flesh.

"All these were given to me, and I am proud of what I have received. And let me add, O Muhammad, that there are more with me than there are with you, and until Doomsday there will be more with me than there are with you."

Then the Prophet said, "If you had not proven what you said with the verses of Allah's book, it would have been hard for me to confirm what you say."

The Devil continued, "Do you know, O

Muhammad, that I have a son whose name is 'Atam [the first third of the night]? He pisses in the ear of the people who go to sleep without performing their night prayers. His urine puts them to sleep; otherwise no one could have gone to bed without finishing their prayers. Then I have a son whose name is *Mutaqadi* [one who presses for payment]. His duty is to publicize the prayers, the devotions, the good deeds that are done in secret for Allah's sake, because Allah promises to reward the good deed done secretly a hundredfold. When deeds are publicized and receive credit and praise from the creatures of Allah, Allah takes away 99 of the promised 100 rewards. Then I have a son whose name is *Kuhayl* [*kohl*]. His duty is to put *kohl* on the eyes of people who are in the presence of the wise or preachers. The ones whose eyes he has touched start falling asleep. They are thus prevented from hearing the words of Allah or receiving any benefit from them."

The Devil talked about women. He said, "Whenever a woman leaves her seat, a devil sits in her place. On the lap of every woman sits a satan who makes her desirable to whoever looks at her. Then he orders the woman to open and show her arms, her legs, and her breasts, and with his claws tears her veil of shame and decency."

Then the Devil started to complain. He said, "O Muhammad, in spite of all this I have no strength to take away the faith of the faithful. I only take away their faith when they throw it away. If I were able, there would be no one on the face of this world who could say *lâ ilâha ill' Allâh, Muhammad rasûlu Llâh* (There is no god but Allah, and Muhammad is His Messenger). I would not leave a single one to pray or fast. All I can do is to give the children of Adam imaginations, illusions, and delusions—make the ugly appear beautiful, the wrong, right, and the bad, good. Neither do you have the power to give faith. You are only a proof of the truth, because I know that if you were given the power to give true faith you would not leave a single nonbeliever on the face of this world.

"The fortunate one who is a believer is fortunate in his mother's womb, and the rebellious sinner is a rebel in his mother's womb. As you are the guide of the fortunate, I am only the cause of sin for the ones who are destined to sin. Allah is He who renders one fortunate and another rebellious." Then he recited

> *And if thy Lord had pleased He would have made people a single nation, and they cease not to differ, except those upon whom thy Lord has mercy, and for this did He create them. And the word of thy Lord is fulfilled: I shall fill Hell with jinn and men altogether.*
>
> (Surah Hûd, 118-119)

And he recited:

> *And the command of Allah is a decree absolute.*
>
> (Surah Ahzab, 38)

Then the Mercy upon the Universe told the Devil, "O Father of All Bitterness, I wonder if it is at all possible for you to repent and return to your Lord. I promise I would intercede for you."

The Accursed One answered, "O Messenger of Allah, it is Allah's justice. The ink on the pen that wrote

244

that judgment is dry. What will happen will happen until Doomsday. The One who made you the master of all the prophets, the speaker for the inhabitants of Paradise, the One who chose you to be the Beloved among all His creation, chose me to be the master of sinners and the speaker for the inhabitants of Hell. He is Allah, devoid of all lack. O Muhammad, this which I have told you is my last word to you, and I have told nothing but the truth."

♦

We take refuge in Allah, the Lord of all the worlds visible and invisible, who existed before and will exist after, from the accursed Devil.

May Allah's peace and blessings be upon our dear master, the Beloved of Allah, His mercy upon the universe; and upon his household and progeny and companions and friends who are loved by him, and upon the ones who love him. ﷺ

SOME SAYINGS OF THE PROPHET

"Real prosperity is not in the abundance of riches
but in contentment."

"Paradise is under the feet of mothers."

"To tell others what one heard about someone,
is sufficient for one as sin."

طَاعَةُ اللهِ طَاعَةُ الْوَالِدِ

"To obey one's parents is like obeying God."

"Action is judged by its result."

"The superiority of men of knowledge over others, is like
my superiority over one of you."

"To withhold knowledge from others is sinful."

"Say 'I believe in God' then be upright."